ASSESSMENT STRATEGIES FOR SELF-DIRECTED LEARNING

EXPERTS IN ASSESSMENT™

SERIES EDITORS

THOMAS R. GUSKEY AND ROBERT J. MARZANO

Please call our toll-free number (800–818–7243)
or visit our website (www.corwinpress.com)
to order individual titles or the entire series.

ASSESSMENT STRATEGIES FOR SELF-DIRECTED LEARNING

ARTHUR L. COSTA AND BENA KALLICK

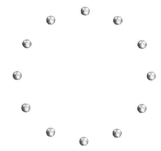

EXPERTS IN ASSESSMENT™

SERIES EDITORS
THOMAS R. GUSKEY AND ROBERT J. MARZANO

CORWIN PRESS
A Sage Publications Company
Thousand Oaks, California

For information:

 Corwin Press
A Sage Publications Company
2455 Teller Road
Thousand Oaks, California 91320
www.corwinpress.com

Sage Publications Ltd.
6 Bonhill Street
London EC2A 4PU
United Kingdom

Sage Publications India Pvt. Ltd.
B-42, Panchsheel Enclave
Post Box 4109
New Delhi 110 017 India

Printed in the United States of America

Library of Congress Cataloging-in-Publication Data

Costa, Arthur L.
Assessment strategies for self-directed learning / by Arthur L. Costa and Bena Kallick.
    p. cm. — (Experts in assessment)
Includes bibliographical references and index.
ISBN 0-7619-3870-2 (cloth) — ISBN 0-7619-3871-0 (pbk.)
    1. Self-culture—Evaluation. I. Kallick, Bena. II. Title. III. Series.
LC32.C66 2004
371.39´43—dc22

                                    2003016725

This book is printed on acid-free paper.

03   04   05   06   10   9   8   7   6   5   4   3   2   1

Acquisitions Editor:	Rachel Livsey
Editorial Assistant:	Phyllis Cappello
Production Editor:	Kristen Gibson
Typesetter:	C&M Digitals (P) Ltd.
Cover Designer:	Tracy E. Miller
Graphic Designer:	Lisa Miller
Copy Editor:	Kris Bergstad
Proofreader:	Eileen Delaney

At this time in history there is a great need for interdependent thinking, problem solving, and flexibility. We dedicate this book to those children in classrooms where their teachers help them invent and build a more thoughtful, humane, and peaceful future.

Contents

Series Editors' Introduction

Standards, assessment, accountability, and grading—these are the issues that dominated discussions of education in the 1990s. Today, they are at the center of every modern education reform effort. As educators turn to the task of implementing these reforms, they face a complex array of questions and concerns that little in their background or previous experience has prepared them to address. This series is designed to help in that challenging task.

In selecting the authors, we went to individuals recognized as true experts in the field. The ideas of these scholar-practitioners have already helped shape current discussions of standards, assessment, accountability, and grading. But equally important, their work reflects a deep understanding of the complexities involved in implementation. As they developed their books for this series, we asked them to extend their thinking, to push the edge, and to present new perspectives on what should be done and how to do it. That is precisely what they did. The books they crafted provide not only cutting-edge perspectives but also practical guidelines for successful implementation.

We have several goals for this series. First, that it be used by teachers, school leaders, policy makers, government officials, and all those concerned with these crucial aspects of education reform. Second, that it helps broaden understanding of the complex issues involved in standards, assessment, accountability, and grading. Third, that it leads to more thoughtful policies and programs. Fourth, and most important, that it helps accomplish the basic goal for which all reform initiatives are intended—namely, to enable all students to learn excellently and to gain the many positive benefits of that success.

Thomas R. Guskey
Robert J. Marzano
Series Editors

"There is only one corner of the universe you can be certain of improving and that's your own self."

Aldous Huxley

Preface

The Wizard of Oz was right when he said to believe in ourselves. . . .
Like Dorothy, we must be true to ourselves and allow others to help us
reveal the answers that are already inside of us.

Brian Koslow

There are many questions about the quality of education and, as is suggested by Koslow, the answers are already inside us. We are certain that we want children to learn to be independent and interdependent, self-initiating learners who strive for excellence and who continue to pursue learning as a lifelong endeavor.

While these educational goals are neither new nor astounding, we were challenged to translate this philosophical rhetoric into practical classroom applications when we developed a videotape course for Lee Canter Associates in 1997 (*Helping Students Become Self-Directed Learners,* 1997). Collaborating with our longtime friend and close associate, Marian Leibowitz, we began to describe the attributes of self-directed learners. We drew upon our previous work on the Habits of Mind (Costa & Kallick, 2000a, 2000b, 2000c, 2000d) and found them to overlap with the dispositions of self-managing, self-monitoring, and self-modifying human beings. What described self-directed learners was also found to be congruent with what we know about efficacious, flexible, interdependent, conscious, problem solvers.

More recently, we have become frustrated with the allure of high-stakes accountability and the emphasis on standardized test scores as the primary tool to assess quality schools, teacher effectiveness, and student achievement. While we value the proper use of data generated from testing, we feel that many politicians and educators have missed the point of what assessment is all about. We believe that the purpose of assessment should be to provide feedback to learners in a process of continual self-improvement. This book is dedicated to those ideals. The purpose is to assist educators in developing school and classroom conditions that support and further students' self-directed learning.

This book is intended to provide support to educators who embrace these ideals. It is intended to strengthen their resolve and to withstand well-intentioned but misguided "innovations" that may build learners who are dependent on others for solutions to problems, who rely on external sources for their motivations, and who turn to others for their goals and aspirations. The book is intended to serve as a practical resource to help educators initiate change, to validate the enhancement of self-directedness as a legitimate goal of education, and to invite critical assessment of emerging school practices for their contributions to the development of students' inner potential. Yet another not-so-hidden agenda is to foster the expansion of this thinking throughout the curriculum, the school, the community, and ultimately the world.

We believe that one powerful contributor to students' continuous learning as a lifelong disposition is energized by assessment. Individuals who are open to feedback from the environment, from themselves, and from others, employ and apply the results of assessment as a source for clarifying their own goals, for establishing their own personal learning, and for self-initiated change. A major purpose of this book, therefore, is to shift the paradigm of assessment from being punitive, summative, and irrelevant both to schools and to the students they serve and, instead, to have assessment as meaningful to learners in their efforts for continual self-enhancement.

School is like the launchpad for a spaceship. All the "life support" systems remain attached until that moment of liftoff when, while it is always in communication with the command center, the spaceship is "on its own." So, too, must we prepare students to take command of themselves; to establish feedback systems for self-guidance; and constantly to monitor their own progress toward their destination, making small maneuvers and midcourse corrections along the way. Similarly, a student's education must provide experiences by which students gradually learn to take charge of their own learning, to become increasingly more aware of their behaviors and their effects on others, and to strengthen their fortitude and resilience to self-correct and self-modify. Thus, the school becomes the launchpad for a life of self-directed learning.

In this volume we provide descriptions of what it looks like and sounds like when students are self-directed in school and classroom settings. We also identify fourteen intellectual dispositions that characterize self-directed learners. While we provide many suggestions for how to infuse self-directed learning throughout the school and classrooms, the information in this volume is not intended to be complete. It is NOT a recipe book, nor does it provide simple answers or immediate solutions to educational dilemmas. Its design is intentionally unfinished and is symbolic of the field of educational inquiry today—controversial, incomplete. Our hope is that it is sufficiently intriguing to instructional leaders as they work with staff, students, and interested community members. Educators need to continue to dialogue, gather additional resources and data, clarify meaning, synthesize definitions, conduct action research, and search for better ways of learning to think through educational problems. Out of this confusion comes enlightenment. Thus the process of developing curriculum, improving instructional strategies, and assessing and reporting on students' growth in the intellectual dispositions of self-directedness is in itself a form of self-directed inquiry and should be an intellectually stimulating experience.

In Chapter 1, we establish the need for learners being self-directed as they face an increasingly complex future. We suggest that self-directedness is an innate force and that education should work to "liberate" that drive that is within every human being. This applies to students as well as teachers. In fact, a prime example of a self-directed learner is the teacher him- or herself. Alone in the classroom, teachers establish goals, draw upon past knowledge, monitor their own actions and those of the students, constantly make midcourse corrections, deal with the ambiguities and uncertainties of classroom life, and, when the lesson is complete, reflect on their behaviors and modify their plans accordingly.

A basic understanding of self-directed learning presented in Chapter 1 is the Feedback Spiral. It is an attempt to diagram how continuous learners set goals, plan for their achievement, execute those plans while gathering data about the achievement of those goals, then reflect on the data and modify their actions accordingly. This concept of Feedback Spirals provides a basic and core concept on which further chapters are built.

Drawing on our earlier works with the Habits of Mind, Chapter 2 includes descriptions of thirteen intellectual dispositions of self-directed learners. We place this in the context of Robert Marzano's helpful model of self-systems thinking and his theories of human motivation.

Chapter 3 focuses on developing students' intellectual capacity for self-assessment. Learning to be self-directed, like developing any other capacity, takes systematic planning, instructional strategies intended to enhance self-directedness, and assessment strategies to determine if students are getting better at it. A variety of assessment strategies and their contributions to self-directed learning are described.

Chapter 4 invites teachers and school staffs to assess themselves, their environment, and their efforts to build self-directedness in others. Is self-directed learning being signaled in the school environment: in our instructional strategies, in our curriculum and assessment practices, and in our reward systems and through our modeling?

Chapter 5 invites teachers to examine their own role and identity. (Nothing is more difficult that to stand back and look critically at our own assumptions, beliefs, and values.) This may require teachers to examine their own "identity" and resolve to modify themselves from "motivators of students" to becoming catalysts for unleashing the motivations with them; from solving others' problems to facilitators of students' learning how to solve problems for themselves, and from evaluators of others to assisting in establishing strategies for gaining feedback through self-evaluation.

Chapter 6 provides some practical suggestions about getting started on your journey toward establishing a school dedicated to self-directed learning. Several schools and teachers who are venturing on this educational pathway provide a wealth of examples from their living it. For their support and contributions we are grateful.

For most people, changing mental models implies the unknown: the psychologically unknown risks of a new venture, the physically unknown demands on time and energy, and the intellectually unknown requirement for new skills and knowledge. Adopting a new vision demands a shift away from our traditional and obsolescent thinking about learning, teaching, achievement, and talent. Changing our mental models will require patience, stamina, and courage.

Mind shifts do not come easily, as they require letting go of old habits, old beliefs, and old traditions. There is a necessary disruption when we shift mental models. If there is not, we are probably not shifting; we may be following new recipes, but we will end up with the same stew! Growth and change are found in "disequilibrium," not balance. Out of chaos, order is built, learning takes place, understandings are built, and, gradually, organizations function more consistently as their vision is clarified, as their mission is forged and their goals operationalized.

In the words of Sylvia Robinson, "Some people think you are strong when you hold on. Others think it is when you let go."

Acknowledgments

W e wish to thank the many students, teachers, and administrators whose valuable contributions made the development of this book possible. They have made the vision of self-directed learning a reality in their districts, schools, and classrooms. Many of their artifacts have been included throughout this volume.

We are fortunate to be a part of a community of learners that includes the many colleagues with whom we work and exchange ideas that stimulate and refine our thinking. We especially acknowledge William Baker, Jane Ellison, Robert Garmston, Carolee Hayes, Heidi Hayes Jacobs, Marian Leibowitz, Laura Lipton, Mary Michailides Richard Strong, and Bruce Wellman.

We wish to thank Tom Guskey and Bob Marzano, the editors, for inviting us to contribute to this series. We appreciate the skills of Kristin Bergstad in editing the manuscript, and thanks to Rachel Livsey, acquisitions editor for Corwin Press, for her encouragement throughout the development of this project.

We also acknowledge the patience and persistence of our spouses, children, and grandchildren. They demonstrated the necessity of applying the dispositions in order to live with two authors.

About the Authors

Arthur L. Costa, Ed.D., is Emeritus Professor of Education at California State University, Sacramento, and co-founder of the Institute for Intelligent Behavior in El Dorado Hills, California. He has served as a classroom teacher, a curriculum consultant, an assistant superintendent for instruction, and as the director of educational programs for the National Aeronautics and Space Administration. He has made presentations and conducted workshops in all fifty states as well as Mexico, Central and South America, Canada, Australia, New Zealand, Africa, Europe, Asia, and the islands of the South Pacific.

Dr. Costa has written numerous books, including *Techniques for Teaching Thinking* (with Larry Lowery), *The School as a Home for the Mind,* and *Cognitive Coaching: A Foundation for Renaissance Schools* (with Robert Garmston). He is editor of *Developing Minds: A Resource Book for Teaching Thinking,* coeditor (with Rosemarie Liebmann) of the *Process as Content Trilogy: Envisioning Process as Content, Supporting the Spirit of Learning,* and *The Process Centered School.* Active in many professional organizations, he served as president of the California Association for Supervision and Curriculum Development and was the National President of the Association for Supervision and Curriculum Development, 1988 to 1989.

Bena Kallick, Ph.D., is a private consultant providing services to school districts, state departments of education, professional organizations, and public sector agencies throughout the United States. She received her doctorate in educational evaluation from Union Graduate School. Her areas of focus include group dynamics, creative and critical thinking, and alternative assessment strategies in the classroom. Formerly a Teachers' Center Director, she also created a children's museum based on problem solving and invention.

Dr. Kallick was the coordinator of a high school alternative designed for at-risk students. Her written work includes "Literature to Think About" (a whole-language curriculum published with Weston Woods Studios), *Changing Schools Into Communities for Thinking,* North

Dakota Study Group, University of North Dakota. She is cofounder of Technology Pathways, a company designed to facilitate teachers' networks and communications about curriculum, instruction, and assessment. Her teaching appointments have included Yale University School of Organization and Management, University of Massachusetts Center for Creative and Critical Thinking, and Union Graduate School. She was on the boards for JOBS for the Future and the Apple Foundation.

Other books coauthored by Arthur Costa and Bena Kallick:

Assessment in the Learning Organization. (1995). Alexandria, VA: Association for Supervision and Curriculum Development.

Habits of Mind: A Developmental Series. (2000).

Book I: Discovering *and Exploring Habits of Mind*

Book II: *Activating and Engaging Habits of Mind*

Book III: *Assessing and Reporting Habits of Mind*

Book IV: *Integrating and Sustaining Habits of Mind*

Alexandria VA: Association for Supervision and Curriculum Development.

Prefatory Statements

A Potato Left Behind

When I was a young lad of about 14 years, my father took me on a summer cross-country auto trip. Along the way, in Iowa, as I recall, we stopped to visit some of his acquaintances who lived in a huge, old farmhouse in a vast, flat field of golden wheat. Because I had never been in such a home as this, our hostess invited me to tour. Tintype photos of grandparents and relatives long since gone, handmade quilts, and antique furniture greeted my curious eyes.

"Would you like to see the root cellar?" she asked. Having never even heard of one, much less seen one, I immediately responded inquisitively. As we descended the wooden stairs, the dank musty smell of earth greeted my nostrils and the darkness required my eyes to adjust. Soon I could make out a bare earthen floor and rock foundation walls lined with shelves supporting dusty glass jars of home-canned produce.

High above the foundation, at ground level, one small window welcomed a beam of sunlight to pierce the darkness. Left behind from the previous winter's storage, a lone potato struggled toward the sun's ray, sending long, white tentacles, leafing pale green only at its farthest tips.

Being at an impressionable age, I marveled at this simple tuber striving to achieve its life's potential—"to become the best potato it could become." Even from this meager environment, this lowly potato managed to find within itself the life force, the "élan," to fulfill its destiny.

From that day, I have always believed that all living things, both plant and animal, have within them a natural, innate vital drive for fulfillment of their potential.

This belief has guided me as an educator dedicated to helping students, teachers, and others find within themselves their inner resources and capabilities. This book is yet another manifestation of my belief that human beings have great capacities for self-direction.

I am convinced that there is a life force within all humans driving them to become self-managing, self-monitoring, and self-modifying.

Arthur L. Costa
Granite Bay, California

A Prefatory Statement From Bena

Everything I need to know about life I learned when my children were growing up. Watching my children develop taught me much about what really matters. For example, one incident that I remember clearly was when our three children were fighting over who was to get the green cup and who the blue cup. They argued, I tried to rationalize, they cried, "It isn't fair." I said, "You're right" and gave them each a cup, regardless of color. Later, upon reflection, I wondered what is meant by "fair." I decided that "fair" meant that each had an equal opportunity. It did not mean "same."

Another powerful experience came from our son when he was in third grade. He had an art teacher he felt was too limiting for his imagination. He came home one day with a mask that he had created. I asked him to tell me about it, what was he trying to express with this object? He described in great detail all of the features that he had played with and how it was supposed to look scary. He then said, "My teacher did not like this but I don't care. She's not the boss of my work." "Not the boss of my work" . . . that resonated. Who owns the work? Who decides whether it is good or bad or if it expresses what it is meant to express?

Finally, when my daughter applied to a college and did not get accepted, she ran to her room in tears. As she ran up the stairs, her brother called out after her, "Just because you were rejected doesn't mean you are a reject."

Each of these instances brings me to the set of questions for this book. How do we create equitable opportunities for students to demonstrate their learning? How do we make certain that the students are the "boss" of their own work? And, finally, how do we make certain that external judgments on their work help them to grow and learn rather than deflating them, leading them to believe that they are "rejects"?

Bena Kallick
Westport, Connecticut

CHAPTER 1

Why We Need Self-Directed Learners

Most states in the United States and several provinces in Canada have imposed extraneous standards for learning. They have implemented externally administered assessments tied to these standards or coupled high school graduation to passing such assessments. Extrinsic accountability links teacher evaluation and even merit pay to increases in test scores. In some states school principals are held accountable for gains in standardized test scores. In the current politics of education, the key to school success is higher test scores. Such practices shift the focus toward the transmission of test-related information, making it difficult to embrace and sustain curriculum and instructional strategies designed for individual meaning-making and personal, self-directed learning. We may be contributing to a generation of "other directed," dependent, externally motivated learners. The basic question is *are we preparing students for a life of tests or for the tests of life?* Or is it possible that, given tests are one of the gatekeepers for a student's future, we should prepare them for both?

If we believe that we are preparing students to strategically confront

> The foundational element in effective work systems is self-correcting, self-managing, self-accountable, self-governing behavior. Energy spent on monitoring and attempting to affect the behavior of team members or other entities from the outside is energy wasted and energy that could be better expended on improving the business and the capability of people. The critical element is to increasingly create self-governing capability.
>
> —Carol Sanford, *Myths of Organizational Effectiveness at Work*

> Children come fully equipped with an insatiable drive to explore and experiment. Unfortunately the primary institutions of our society are oriented predominantly toward controlling rather than learning, rewarding individuals for performing for others rather than cultivating their natural curiosity and impulse to learn.
>
> —Peter Senge, "The Leader's New Work"

and creatively resolve the ambiguous, paradoxical, and dichotomous problems and conflicts they will encounter in our increasingly more complex society, then the focus of education must shift. Both teachers and students must become continual and internally driven learners: self-analyzing, self-referencing, self-evaluating, and self-correcting. The purpose of this book is to establish a refreshing new view of assessment practices and to illuminate how assessment can enhance continuous, lifelong, self-directed learning.

Assessing as an Essential Component of Learning

Technology is now driving a new definition of accountability. We have the capacity to track data with greater specificity, thereby providing better information to teachers about test results. State departments are becoming increasingly more astute about how to provide such information. However, given the number of tests that are being given, the cost of such procedures, and the lack of timeliness from most state departments, analysis of results does not always provide good individual diagnostic information.

> You have the power to declare the person you are becoming.
>
> —Joe Marino

In addition, process-oriented goals, such as the student's capability to become more self-directed and self-evaluative, cannot be assessed using product-oriented measurement techniques. Our existing evaluation paradigm must therefore shift to one that allows for a more balanced method that includes classroom-based assessments that complement state-based assessments. Assessing student growth toward self-direction demands alternative and authentic forms of assessment. Students can become more self-directed when they know the intended learning outcomes and receive constructive feedback regarding their progress during the learning process. Alternate and more authentic forms of assessment are performance based, including rubrics, checklists, portfolios, and exhibitions that allow students to demonstrate their understanding and application of knowledge through the creation of a product or performance.

We believe that assessment is a mechanism for providing ongoing feedback to the learner and to the organization as a necessary part of the spiraling processes of continuous renewal: self-managing, self-monitoring, and self-modifying. We must constantly remind ourselves that the ultimate purpose of evaluation is to have students learn to become self-evaluative. When students graduate from our schools, we want them to have methods of self-evaluation and to know how to turn to external critique for self-improvement. We want them to know how to give and receive constructive feedback and how to revise their work based on such feedback. If students graduate from our schools dependent on others without an understanding of what is good, adequate, or excellent work, then we have failed them.

Evaluation, the highest level in Bloom's Taxonomy (1956), means generating, holding in your head, and applying a set of internal and external criteria. For too long, teachers have been practicing that skill. We need to shift that responsibility to students—to help them develop the capacity for self-analysis, self-referencing, and self-modification.

We believe that the intent of assessment should be to support learners in becoming self-directing and that what matters most in any assessment strategy is whether learners are becoming increasingly more able to self-evaluate. We want students to know how to give, receive, and make good use of constructive feedback.

Self-knowledge is the first step in self-assessment. The intent of this book is to provide educators with strategies to design diverse ways of gathering, organizing, and reporting evidence of continual learning and meaning-making in their efforts to support learners in becoming self-managing, self-monitoring, and self-modifying.

The Demand for Self-Directed Learners

Simply teaching students how to read the bible was once a sufficient mission for schools. Modern educators are realizing, however, that new goals are becoming increasingly apparent as survival skills for our children's future, for the perpetua-

> You might well remember that nothing can bring you success but yourself.
>
> —Napoleon Hill

tion of our democratic institutions, and even for our planetary existence (Hay, 2001). Such goals include the following:

- The capacity for continued learning
- Knowing how to behave when answers to problems are not immediately apparent

- Cooperativeness and team building
- Precise communication in a variety of modes
- The appreciation of disparate value systems
- Problem solving that requires creativity and ingenuity
- The enjoyment of resolving ambiguous, discrepant, and paradoxical situations
- The generation and organization of an overabundance of technologically produced information
- The pride and craftsmanship of product
- Knowing and accepting ourselves
- Personal commitment to larger organizational and global values

Dave Posner, chief technical officer of Encirq Corporation, states, "What our 21st Century citizens need are trained minds and a passion for creative endeavor. And by a 'trained mind' I mean not only the ability to think, to gather data, to formulate models, to test hypotheses, to reason to conclusions, and so on. I mean, most importantly, the desire for and habit of thinking."

Business leaders warn that the workforce must undergo a revolutionary change in order to respond effectively to this new work environment. Workers have to rethink their approach to "work" as they previously knew it. They are focusing more on learning how to build values, attitudes, and skills that will allow them to survive and succeed through multiple job changes and with far less structure and security (Panella, 1997). Dent (1995) states, "The coming work revolution will force us to rediscover our greatest strength—individual initiative— thus nurturing a spirit of entrepreneurship."

A person's sense of self-efficacy—believing that you have the capacity to do the job—is the most influential factor in ensuring a person's success in life. Bandura (1997) states,

> Perceived self-efficacy is concerned not with the number of skills you have, but with what you believe you can do with what you have under a variety of circumstances . . . effective functioning requires both skills and the efficacy beliefs to use them well.

Our democracy is threatened by a lack of commitment to citizenship, particularly the right to vote. We are exposed to so many sources of information that it has been increasingly more difficult to determine whether sources are credible. Our students will have to learn how to read information and discern the biases. They will have to become better informed about the global as well as local impact that the government's decisions will have. Our democracy is based on the principles of balance—a delicate balance between local, state, and nation. Now, more than ever, we must protect that balance through the constant vigilance of our citizenship. Students will have to know how to develop and defend their opinions based on the information they absorb. This requires continuous self-directed learning.

People governed by an internal locus of control show initiative in controlling their environment. They control their own impulsivity, gather information, are cognitively active, eagerly learn information that will increase their probability for success, and show signs of humor. When compared with individuals with an external locus of control, they are less anxious, less hostile, less angry, more trustful, less suspicious of others, less prone to suicide, less depressed, and less prone to psychosis (Laborde & Saunders, 1986).

Self-Direction: A Natural Human Tendency

Humans quest for mastery of their environment, control, self-empowerment, and continuous lifelong learning. Wheatley and Kellner-Rogers (1998) state,

> Each human being is bred with a unique set of potentials that yearn to be fulfilled as surely as the acorn yearns to become the oak within it.
>
> —Aristotle

> Every living thing acts to develop and preserve itself. Identity is the filter that every organism or system uses to make sense of the world. New information, new relationships, changing environments—all are interpreted through a sense of self. This tendency toward self-creation is so strong that it creates a seeming paradox. An organism will change to maintain its identity.

Peak performers' primary locus of control is not external, but internal. One element that stands out clearly among peak performers is their virtually unassailable belief in the likelihood of their own success—and their track records reinforce their beliefs (Garfield, 1995).

Recent research in the neurosciences indicates that the human brain reconstructs itself from experience. Ornstein claims, "To make a personal change, we have to be able to observe the automatic workings inside ourselves. He describes the brain as having a neural selection system that wires up the nervous system differently, depending on the demands on the organism." Managing and developing the mind is to bring automatic processes into consciousness.

Defining Self-Directedness

A self-directed person can be described as being

- *Self-Managing:* Knowing the significance of and being inclined to approach tasks with a sense of clarity about the outcomes, a strategic plan, and necessary data, and then drawing from past experiences, anticipating success indicators, and creating alternatives for accomplishment
- *Self-Monitoring:* Having sufficient self-knowledge about what works, establishing conscious metacognitive strategies to alert the perceptions for in-the-moment indicators of whether the strategic plan is working or not, and to assist in the decision-making processes of altering the plan and choosing the right actions and strategies
- *Self-Modifying:* Reflecting on, evaluating, analyzing, and constructing meaning from experience and applying the learning to future activities, tasks, and challenges

These dispositions transcend all subject matters commonly taught in school. They are characteristic of peak performers whether they be in homes, schools, athletic fields, organizations, the military, governments, churches, or corporations. They are what make marriages successful, learning continual, workplaces productive, and democracies enduring.

> Authenticity necessitates behaving autonomously, for it means being the author of one's actions—acting in accord with one's true inner self.
>
> —Edward Deci, *Why We Do What We Do*

The goal of education, therefore, should be to support others and ourselves in liberating, developing, and habituating these intellectual dispositions more fully. Taken together, they are a force directing us toward increasingly authentic, congruent, ethical behavior, the touchstones of integrity. They are the tools of disciplined choice making. They are the primary vehicles in the lifelong journey toward integration. They are the "right stuff" that makes human beings efficacious.

Assessing the "Bigger Picture"

Since the school environment and culture signals their values, teachers will more likely value and teach for self-directed learning if they are in an environment that models, supports, and values self-directed learning. Teachers who have a sense of efficacy spawn more efficacious learners. No assessment of any one unit is complete, therefore, without assessing the qualities of the other surrounding units. To assess student progress, the quality of classroom conditions must be monitored as well. To assess teacher performance, the quality of school workplace conditions must be examined; and to assess the quality of the school district, the community support and commitment must also be assessed. Thus, a well-conceived assessment design includes a search for consistency and integrity of surrounding conditions that directly influence each component of the organization. Through sound leadership practices, staff development, and coaching, all inhabitants of the learning organization can become continuous and self-directed learners.

> How much do students really love to learn, to persist, to passionately attack a problem or a task?
>
> . . . to watch some of their prized ideas explode and to start anew?
>
> . . . to go beyond being merely dutiful or long-winded?
>
> Let us assess such things.
>
> —Grant Wiggins

Learning Continuously Through Feedback Spirals

Self-directed learners demonstrate a commitment to change by building critique and assessment into their everyday actions. By reexamining and clarifying various aspects of the values, purposes, goals, strategies, and outcomes, they continue to learn and develop an even more positive disposition toward continued learning. But what process design best promotes this kind of feedback and continuous learning? Individuals employ feedback spirals by scanning the environment for clues about the results of their actions.

> Whoever ceases to be a student has never been a student.
>
> —George Iles

Components of Feedback Spirals

Feedback spirals depend on a variety of information for their success. In some cases, individuals make changes after consciously observing and reflecting on their own feelings, attitudes, and skills. Some spirals depend on the observations of outsiders (critical friends). And in other cases, those directly involved in a change collect specific kinds of evidence about what is happening in the organization's environment. Once these data are analyzed, interpreted, and internalized, actions are modified to more closely achieve the goals. Thus, individuals are continually self-learning, self-renewing, and self-modifying.

The components of a feedback spiral may be diagrammed as a recursive, cyclical pathway (Figure 1.1):

Clarify goals and purposes: What is the purpose for what you are doing? What beliefs or values does it reflect? What outcomes would you expect as a result of your actions?

Planning: What actions would you take to achieve the desired outcomes? How would you set up an experiment to test your ideas? What evidence would you collect to help to inform you about the results of your actions? What would you look for as indicators your outcomes were or were not achieved? And how will you leave the door open for other discoveries and possibilities that were not built into the original design? What process will you put in place that will help you describe what actually happened?

Take action/implement: Execute the plan

Assess/gather evidence: Implement the assessment strategy

Study, reflect, evaluate/derive meaning: Whether this is an individual or organizational change, how are the results congruent with stated values? What meaning can be made of the data? Who might serve as critical friends to coach, facilitate, or mediate your learning from this experience? What have you learned from this action?

Modify actions based on new knowledge: What will be done differently in the future as a result of reflection and integration of new knowledge? Is this worth trying again?

Revisit/redefine: Do the goals still make sense? Are they still of value or do they need to be redefined, refocused, refined? This returns to the first step in the spiral of goal clarification.

The Teacher as a Self-Directed, Continuous Learner

The concept of self-directed learning is familiar to many professional teachers. As they are self-directed, learning includes self-managing,

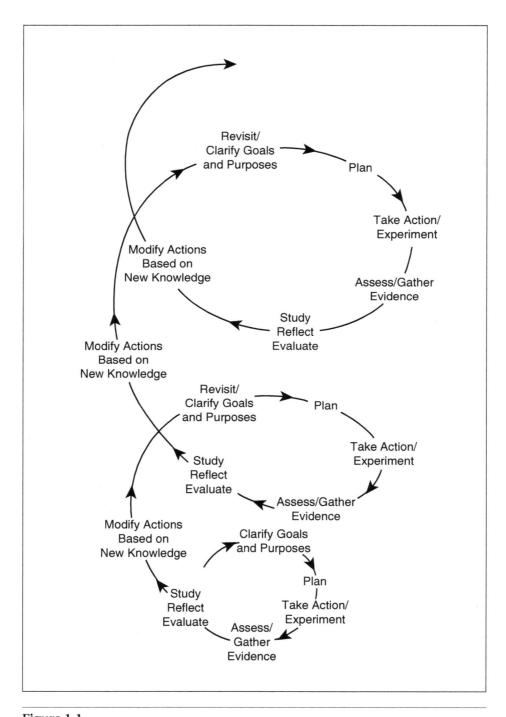

Figure 1.1

SOURCE: Costa & Kallick (1994), *Assessment in the learning organization*. Alexandria, VA: Association for Supervision and Curriculum Development. Used by permission.

self-monitoring, and self-modifying. These behaviors apply as much to teachers as they do to students.

Teachers self-manage, self-monitor, and self-modify on a daily basis. They plan lessons, activities, units, and events intended to produce student learning. During an event or lesson, teachers keep that plan in mind and continually monitor their own and student's behaviors, being alert to indicators of achievement. Then, upon completion of the lesson, teachers reflect on the lesson to evaluate its effectiveness in producing the desired student outcomes. Thus, the act of teaching is viewed as an opportunity for continually improving student learning and the craft of teaching.

As you read and reflect on this section, you may better understand what is meant by self-directed learning as it is applied to our craft of teaching. You are also invited to assess your professional self by comparing what effective teachers do with your own instructional dispositions and capacities.

The Self-Managing Teacher

Prior to teaching, most teachers engage in the complex intellectual skills of planning. Such teacher decisions include the following:

Becoming clear and precise about descriptions of anticipated student learnings that are predicted as a result of instruction. During planning, a teacher envisions cues: definitions of acceptable forms of student performance for learning. The teacher also selects potential solutions, back-up procedures, and alternative strategies for times when the activity needs to be redirected. Accomplished teachers have immediate goals for a lesson, but they also know that the lesson leads to a longer-term, more pervasive outcome as well. They keep in mind the school's or district's standards of learning.

Drawing forth past knowledge about students' present capabilities or entry knowledge. This information is drawn from previous teaching and learning experiences, data from school records, test scores, and clues from previous teachers, parents, and counselors. Empathic teachers plan lessons taking the students' point of view—their interests, their attention span, and learning styles.

Making mental maps of the instructional sequences or strategies that will most likely produce immediate and long-range instructional outcomes. Flexible teachers draw on multiple strategies to achieve their lesson goals. Based on their knowledge of the content to be taught, the learners in their charge, and the available resources, they can design multiple alternative instructional strategies for achieving their goals. (This becomes even more apparent during teaching—the self-monitoring—described below.)

Anticipating strategies for assessing student outcomes. Gathering evidence during the lesson will provide a basis for evaluating and making decisions about the design of future instruction.

Planning for continuous self-learning. Self-directed teachers view each lesson as a "thought experiment" in which not only the students learn but so, too, does the teacher. Every lesson provides an opportunity to learn more about the craft of teaching and instructional strategies, the processes of student learning, the content or discipline in which they are working, or the standards of learning. For example, as a continuous learner, the teacher might say to him- or herself: "I'm experimenting with my wait time after asking a question; I'm going to pay attention to what happens to students' thinking when I increase my use of wait time." Or, "In our staff development, I learned about asking more complex questions using positive presuppositions. Today this lesson will provide a perfect opportunity to practice designing and posing those complex questions and to search for their effects on my students."

Sometimes events happen in the classroom to which teachers spontaneously and intuitively respond. Even though these actions are unplanned, they can serve as a source of continuous learning as well. Teachers might "take a birdwalk" from their designed lesson and students get so intrigued that the results are better than what was planned. The teacher may then add that strategy to his or her repertoire and plan to use it again.

Planning flexibly with the student in mind. Planning also demands that the teacher think flexibly by engaging multiple student perspectives, multiple and simultaneous outcomes, and multiple pathways. Effective teachers have the capacity to view their lesson in both the immediate and longer range as well as from their own and students' points of view. They are not only analytical about the details of this lesson and can also see connections between this lesson and other related learnings. They know where this lesson is leading and how it is connected to broader curriculum goals.

The Self-Monitoring Teacher

Once a lesson begins, effective teachers are alert, aware, and conscious of what is occurring in the classroom. Most teachers have little time to consider alternative teaching strategies and the consequences of each. During the lesson, teachers constantly make conscious or subconscious, spontaneous, and planned decisions.

Keeping standards of learning and a planned strategy in mind while teaching provides teachers with a backdrop against which to make new decisions. One of the great mental skills of teaching is to remember the lesson plan during the press of interaction. Teachers often suffer cognitive overload: too many things going on all at the same time.

Metacognitive teachers are aware of their own thinking, decisions, and actions. *Metacognition* refers to teachers' critically important capacities to consciously "stand outside themselves" and reflect on themselves as they manage instruction. During a lesson, teachers may ask themselves, "Are my directions clear? Can students see the image on the screen? Am I communicating precisely so students understand me? Should I speed up?" Such internal dialogue means the teacher is constantly monitoring his or her own and students' behavior during instruction.

Successful, conscious teachers engage in such metacognitive skills as the following:

- Keeping place in a long sequence of operations
- Knowing that a subgoal has been attained
- Detecting errors and recovering from them by making a quick fix or retreating to the last known correct operation

This kind of monitoring involves both looking ahead and looking back. Looking ahead includes

- Learning the structure of a sequence of operations and identifying areas where errors are likely
- Choosing a strategy that will reduce the possibility of error and will provide easy recovery
- Identifying the kinds of feedback that will be available at various points and evaluating the usefulness of that feedback

Looking back includes

- Detecting errors previously made
- Keeping a history of what has been done to the present and thereby what should come next
- Assessing the reasonableness of the present and the immediate outcome of task performance

Flexible teachers manage their impulsivity by avoiding strong emotional reactions to classroom events. This is an efficient strategy to reserve the limited capacity for conscious processing of immediate classroom decisions.

Many classes are filled with students in a heterogeneous array of languages, cultures, and learning styles. Each student must be dealt with employing different strategies, cultural experiences, vocabulary, examples, and techniques. Flexible teachers have a vast repertoire of instructional strategies and techniques, and they call forth alternative strategies as needed (Costa & Garmston, 2000, pp. 163-167).

The Self-Modifying Teacher

After teaching the lesson, the teacher now has two sources of information: the lesson that was envisioned during planning and the actual lesson as performed. Teachers analyze the lesson by collecting and using understandings derived from the comparison between actual and intended outcomes. If the teacher finds a great similarity between the two, there is a match. But a discrepancy exists when there is a mismatch between what was observed and what was planned. Teachers generate reasons to explain the discrepancy: cause-and-effect relationships between instructional situations and behavioral outcomes.

Self-directed teachers take responsibility for their own actions and constantly strive to improve. One might hear a self-evaluating teacher say, "Of course the students were confused. Did you hear my directions? They were all garbled. I've got to give more precise directions."

Self-directed teachers consciously reflect upon, conceptualize, and apply understandings from one classroom experience to the next. As a result of this analysis and reflection they synthesize new knowledge about teaching and learning. As experiences with teaching and learning accumulate, concepts are derived and constructed. Teachers' practice thus becomes more routinized, particularized, and refined. They are capable of predicting consequences of their decisions and experiment more and take more risks. They expand their repertoire of techniques and strategies to be used in different settings with varying content and unique students and situations.

Thus, the professional teacher is a continual learner—managing the instruction and learning in their classrooms, self-monitoring their own and students behaviors, and then self-modifying to improve themselves and their students' achievement constantly.

A Reflection on Learning

Following is a reflection by Heather Wieler, a second-grade teacher at Glenora Elementary School in Edmonton, Canada:

Initially I thought the students would respond to the choice with confusion—thinking they had to do them all or feeling confused about "which one to choose." However, I found that when given clear expectations and examples of another's work they were very enthusiastic about the project. I also realized that my students have become familiar and comfortable with the idea that not everything has to be done the same way by everyone all the time. They are starting to realize that there are often different ways of solving the same problem or different strategies that can be used to accomplish the same task. In this lesson they were excited to choose what they really wanted to reflect on—instead of being told what to reflect on. I was also surprised at the quality of writing I received from the children. They knew they had to follow the criteria, but the content was up to them and it was evident in their writing. I received entries that were meaningful, perceptive, detailed and insightful—and perhaps what was most intriguing was that each entry was so unique. I didn't read the same thing over twenty-six times but was genuinely interested in what the children had to say because they wrote about what was meaningful to them.

As we read through the examples together I asked the students questions such as

Where did this person use "think back"?

What details is he giving?

Can you find the sentence with the details?

How about the looking ahead part?

The students enthusiastically identified parts where the writer was using "Think back . . . Look ahead." However, they missed a key example I was hoping they would find—they did not make the connection that the one person wrote about how working in a greenhouse is important to the community and that was a concept discussed in the previous social unit. I considered pointing it out—but decided instead to let them find their own examples of evaluation and see where their own observations took them. It's still a learning process for me too—that there isn't always one right "answer" or way of doing things. It's not self-directed learning when you simply tell students everything—we have to let them make the discoveries.

My objective in getting the students to use the motto "Think back . . . Look ahead" and to identify examples of evaluation is to get them to articulate the thinking that they do. It is a learning process for them and for us as teachers—but as we continue our work with our students it is amazing to see the growth from year to year in both the staff and students.

Summary

To develop the humility of continuous learning, the school community gathers data through conscious observation of their own feelings, attitudes, and skills; through observation and interviews with others; and through collecting evidence of the effects of their efforts on the environment. These data are analyzed, interpreted, internalized. Based on this analysis, actions are modified in order to achieve the goals more closely. Thus, individuals and organization are continually self-learning, self-renewing, and self-modifying (Costa & Kallick, 1994).

Self-directed people are resourceful. They tend to engage in cause-and-effect thinking, spend energy on tasks, set challenging goals, persevere in the face of barriers and occasional failures, and accurately forecast future performances. They proactively locate resources when perplexed. Seeking constant improvement, they are flexible in their perspectives and are optimistic and confident with self-knowledge.

Self-directed people are in a continuous learning mode. Their confidence, in combination with their inquisitiveness, allows them to constantly search for new and better ways. People with this disposition are always striving for improvement, always growing, always learning, always modifying and improving themselves. They seize problems, situations, tensions, conflicts, and circumstances as valuable opportunities to learn.

A great mystery about humans is that we confront learning opportunities with fear rather than curiosity and wonder. We seem to feel better when we know rather than when we learn. We defend our biases, beliefs, and storehouses of knowledge rather than inviting the unknown, the creative, and the inspirational. Being certain and closed gives us comfort while being doubtful and open gives us fear.

Immersed from an early age in a curriculum of fragmentation, competition, and reaction, students are trained to believe that deep learning means figuring out the right answer rather than developing capabilities for effective and thoughtful action. They have been taught to value certainty rather than doubt, to give answers rather than to inquire, to know which choice is correct rather than to explore alternatives.

Our wish is for creative students and people who are eager to learn. That includes the humility of knowing that we don't know, which is the highest form of thinking we will ever learn. Paradoxically, unless you start off with humility you will never get anywhere, so as the first step you already have to have what will eventually be the crowning glory of all learning: the humility to know—and admit—that you don't know and not be afraid to find out. This book will show how self-assessment contributes to such growth.

Organization of the Remainder of This Book

In Chapter 2 we describe the dispositions of self-directed learners. We start by building a background based on Robert Marzano's (2001) *New Taxonomy of Educational Objectives*. We then describe fourteen intellectual dispositions of self-directed learners. These dispositions often overlap as they are intended to be performed in an integrated way. They are classified under three components of self-directedness: self-managing, self-monitoring, and self-modifying.

Promoting self-directed learning doesn't "just happen" because we believe in it. It must become an integral component of the curriculum, instruction, assessment, and the culture of the learning organization. Everyone in the school community needs to continue to develop their capacities for self-directedness in order to build a community dedicated to continuous learning, incorporating many examples from schools that are dedicated to self-directed learning. Chapter 3 provides a range and variety of assessment strategies, all with the intent of promoting self-directed learning. Incorrect application of traditional forms of assessment may be used as summative and even punitive. This chapter shows how assessment may be used as a tool for students to gather data about their own progress, how assessment may promote personal mastery, and how feedback energizes continual learning.

What district, school, and classroom conditions must be in place for learners to become self-directed? Chapter 4 describes those cultural elements and the leadership qualities needed to construct and signal self-directed learning as a valid outcome for all the inhabitants of the learning community.

Peter Senge (Newcomb, 2003) believes that "to educate children well, school superintendents and cafeteria workers alike need to scrutinize how they think about their jobs. They must become aware of the deeply ingrained assumptions they may not even know they have—but that can inhibit their performance or blind them to new possibilities."

The teacher's role is crucial. This means that many teachers must modify their approaches from a traditional approach where information is dispensed and judged to one of inquirer, questioner, facilitator, and model. With the constant intention of having the student in charge of his or her own learning, we investigate the decision-making processes of teaching as lessons are designed, content selected, and instruction performed. Changing our ways of teaching to facilitate student self-directed learning may take a perceptual shift for many of us—from teacher as problem solver to assisting students to solve their own problems; from feeling solely responsible for motivating students to unleashing the innate motivation students have to learn; and from using praise and rewards to motivate learning to helping students gain satisfaction for themselves for achieving their goals.

> Success isn't a result of spontaneous combustion. You must set yourself on fire.
>
> —Arnold H. Glasow

OK, so now you're convinced that schools and teachers should embrace self-directed learning. Where to begin? Drawing on experiences from other successful schools, Chapter 6 offers many suggestions for how to mobilize for action, how to get started, and where to begin.

The appendices include additional resources to support your new journey. They have further references and materials as well as quotations that exemplify self-directed learning.

CHAPTER 2

The Intellectual Dispositions of Self-Directed Learners

O ne of the distinguishing characteristics between humans and other forms of life is our inclination and ability to *find* problems to solve. By definition, a problem is any stimulus, task, phenomenon, or discrepancy, the explanation for which is not immediately known. When we as humans experience dichotomies, are confused by dilemmas, or come face to face with uncertainties—our most effective actions require drawing forth certain patterns of intellectual behavior to resolve the discrepancies. What is unique about self-directed people is their capacity to draw forth certain intellectual dispositions under challenging conditions. When they encounter and engage in resolving these problems, self-directed people are intrigued by and lend themselves to resolving challenging situations. They display their capacities for strategic reasoning, insightfulness, perseverance, creativity, and craftsmanship. Through reflection, they construct meaning from their experiences and accumulate strategies, maps, and procedures that are then applied in future problem-solving situations.[1]

Marzano's Model

Marzano (2001) describes a useful theoretical model for how human beings confront tasks. He refers to the following:

Self-System Thinking: This consists of an interrelated system of attitudes, beliefs, and emotions that determines both motivation and attention. Marzano suggests that when a person encounters a task, the "self-system" is the first to be engaged. Based upon beliefs and goals, judgments are made about the advisability of engaging in the task. The self-system determines the motivation necessary to perform and learn from engaging in the task. If the task is judged important, if the probability of success is high, and positive effect is generated or associated with the task, there will be motivation to engage in the task.

Metacognitive System: If the decision is made to engage in the problem or task, the next system, the metacognitive system, sets the goals and designs strategies for accomplishing the goals.

Cognitive System: The effectiveness of the processing of the information that is essential for task accomplishment is the responsibility of the cognitive system. This includes such cognitive processes as making inferences, comparing, classifying, and sequencing.

Knowledge: The success of any task accomplishment is dependent on the amount of knowledge and prior experience an individual brings to the task (Marzano, 2001).

What Motivates Self-Directed Learners?

Marzano claims that the interaction among an individual's attitudes, beliefs, and emotions determines the motivation and attention one gives to solving problems or accomplishing complex tasks. He suggests that there are four types of self-system thinking that contribute to one's motivation to resolve problems or mounting complex tasks. They are: importance, efficacy, emotional response, and overall motivation.

By *importance,* Marzano suggests that the task be perceived as instrumental in attaining a personal goal or satisfying a basic need. Self-directed people would choose to engage in a task based on how important the task is to them.

Efficacy means having the resources, ability, or power to change a situation. Self-directed persons would assess the availability of resources, and examine their own skills and competencies to bring to this task or problematic situation. If the motivation were strong enough, self-directed persons would take steps to acquire the competencies and skills to perform the task well.

Emotions are primary motivators. They sometimes are more powerful influences on our actions than are beliefs about efficacy and our values about what is important. Being aware of their emotions, self-directed people analyze the extent to which their emotional response to a given situation is influencing their motivation.

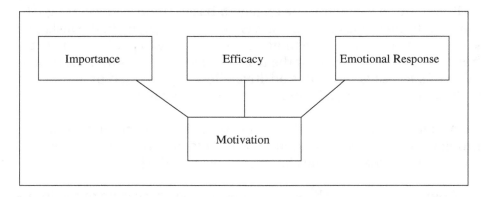

Figure 2.1   Aspects of Motivation

SOURCE: Reprinted from *Designing a New Taxonomy of Educational Objectives* by Robert J. Marzano (2001).

Self-directed learners are those who, rather than avoiding problems, enjoy them and even seek out problems to solve. They know how to confront problems with confidence and strategic approaches, setting realistic and clear goals and designing strategies to achieve their goals. They consciously monitor the effectiveness of their problem-solving strategies and employ alternatives if they find them lacking. They monitor the clarity of their goals, the accuracy and fidelity of their products, and the effectiveness of the strategies they employ to resolve their problems and to achieve their goals. They are aware of their own behaviors and the effects of their actions on others and the environment. They draw forth knowledge and experiences from their past to inform their actions. They learn from their problem-solving experiences, modify their behaviors accordingly, and transfer and apply their learnings in other novel situations.

We will describe the intellectual dispositions of effective, self-directed learners as they confront challenges to resolve, manage their decisions to perform tasks, and solve problems.

Intellectual Dispositions

The intellectual dispositions of self-directed people are performed in response to those questions and problems whose answers are NOT immediately known. The results that are produced by the application of these intellectual resources are more powerful, of higher quality, and of greater significance than if those intellectual dispositions were not employed. A critical attribute of self-directed human beings is not only having information, but also knowing how to act on it.

Employing intellectual dispositions requires a composite of many skills, attitudes, cues, past experiences, and proclivities. It means that we value one pattern of thinking over another and it therefore implies making a choice about which pattern should be employed at this time. It includes alertness to the contextual cues that signal this as an appropriate time and circumstance in which the employment of this pattern would be useful. It requires a level of skillfulness to employ and carry through the behaviors effectively over time. It suggests that as a result of each experience in which these behaviors were employed, the effects of their use are reflected upon, evaluated, modified, and carried forth to future applications.

We described self-directed people as follows:

- *1. Self-Managing:* Approaching tasks with clarity of outcomes, a strategic plan, and necessary data, and then drawing from past experiences, anticipating success indicators, and creating alternatives for accomplishment.
- *2. Self-Monitoring:* Establishing metacognitive strategies to alert the perceptions for in-the-moment indicators of whether the strategic plan is working or not and to assist in the decision-making processes of altering the plan.
- *3. Self-Modifying:* Reflecting on, evaluating, analyzing, and constructing meaning from the experience and applying the learning to future activities, tasks, and challenges.

While these three components are listed and will be described in the above order, it does not imply that they are performed in this sequence. All three of these attributes may occur simultaneously.

In this chapter we more specifically describe the types of behaviors and intellectual patterns that self-directed people display. The intent is to provide staff, students, and the learning community with a common vision of what it means to be self-directed, how self-directedness may be cultivated, and how growth toward greater self-directedness may be assessed. Our goals are to

- Encourage schools and communities to elevate their level and broaden their scope of curricular outcomes by focusing on self-directed learning as an enduring and lifelong quest
- Enhance instructional decision making to employ content, not as an end of instruction, but rather as a vehicle for becoming more self-directed

- Learn about a range of techniques and strategies for gathering evidence of growth in students' self-directed learning
- Use feedback not only to guide students to become self-assessing but also for school teams and parents to use assessment data for continuous improvement
- Forge a common vision among all members of the educational community of what characterizes self-directed learners

Self-Managing

The Management of Impulsivity

Self-directed people have a sense of deliberativeness: They think before they act. They intentionally form a vision of a product, plan of action, goal, or destination before they begin. They strive to clarify and understand directions, develop a strategy for approaching a problem, and withhold immediate value judgments until fully understanding an idea. Reflective individuals consider alternatives and consequences of several possible directions prior to taking action. They decrease their need for trial and error by gathering information, taking time to reflect on an answer before giving it, making sure they understand directions, and listening to alternative points of view.

> Goal directed self-imposed delay of gratification is perhaps the essence of emotional self-regulation: the ability to deny impulse in the service of a goal, whether it be building a business, solving an algebraic equation, or pursuing the Stanley Cup.
>
> —Daniel Goleman, *Emotional Intelligence* (1995)

Often students blurt out the first answer that comes to mind. Sometimes they shout out an answer, start to work without fully understanding the directions, and lack an organized plan or strategy for approaching a problem. They may take the first suggestion given or operate on the most obvious and simple idea that comes to mind rather than considering more complex alternatives and the consequences of several possible directions.

Thinking Flexibly

An amazing discovery about the human brain is its plasticity—its ability to "rewire," change, and even repair itself to become smarter. Flexible people are the ones with the most control. They have the capacity to change their mind as they receive additional data. They engage in multiple and simultaneous outcomes and activities, draw upon a repertoire of problem-solving strategies, and can practice style flexibility, knowing when it is appropriate to be broad and global in their

> If you never change your mind, why have one?
>
> —Edward deBono

thinking and when a situation requires detailed precision. They create and seek novel approaches and have a well-developed sense of humor. They envision a range of consequences.

Flexible people can approach a problem from a new angle using a novel approach (deBono, 1970, refers to this as *lateral thinking)*. They consider alternative points of view or deal with several sources of information simultaneously. Their minds are open to change based on additional information and data or reasoning that contradicts their beliefs. Flexible people know that they have and can develop options and alternatives to consider. They understand means–end relationships, are able to work within rules, criteria, and regulations, and they can predict the consequences of flouting them. They understand not only the immediate reactions but are also able to perceive the bigger purposes that such constraints serve. Thus, flexibility of mind is essential for working with social diversity, enabling an individual to recognize the wholeness and distinctness of other people's ways of experiencing and making meaning.

Flexible thinkers are able to shift, at will, through multiple perceptual positions. One perceptual orientation is what Jean Piaget called *egocentrism*—perceiving from our own point of view. By contrast, *allocentrism* is the position in which we perceive through another person's orientation. We operate from this second position when we empathize with other's feelings, predict how others are thinking, and anticipate potential misunderstandings.

Another perceptual position is "macrocentric." It is similar to looking down from a balcony at ourselves and our interactions with others. This bird's-eye view is useful for discerning themes and patterns across assortments of information. It is intuitive, holistic, and conceptual. Since we often have incomplete information for solving problems, we need the capacity to perceive general patterns and jump across gaps when knowledge is incomplete or when some of the pieces are missing.

Yet another perceptual orientation is microcentric—examining the individual and sometimes minute parts that make up the whole. This "worm's-eye view," without which science, technology, and any complex enterprise could not function, involves logical analytical computation and searching for causality in methodical steps. It requires attention to detail, precision, and orderly progressions.

Flexible thinkers display confidence in their intuition. They tolerate confusion and ambiguity up to a point, and are willing to let go of a problem, trusting their subconscious to continue creative and productive work on it. Flexibility is the cradle of humor, creativity, and repertoire. While there are many possible perceptual positions—past, present, future, egocentric, allocentric, macrocentric, visual, auditory, kinesthetic—the flexible mind is activated by knowing when to shift perceptual positions.

Some students have difficulty in considering alternative points of view or dealing with more than one classification system simultaneously. THEIR way to solve a problem seems to be the ONLY way. They perceive situations from a very ego-centered point of view: "My way or the highway!" Their mind is made up; "Don't confuse me with facts, that's it."

Questioning

Effective problem solvers know how to ask questions to fill in the gaps between what they know and what they don't know. Effective questioners are inclined to ask a range of questions. For example: requests for data to support others' conclusions and assumptions—such questions as,

"What evidence do you have that . . . ?"

"How do you know that's true?"

"How reliable is this data source?"

They pose questions about alternative points of view:

"From whose viewpoint are we seeing, reading, or hearing?"

"From what angle, what perspective are we viewing this situation?"

Students pose questions that make causal connections and relationships:

"How are these people (events) (situations) related to each other?"

"What produced this connection?"

They pose hypothetical problems characterized by "iffy"-type questions:

"What do you think would happen IF . . . ?"

"IF that is true, then what might happen when . . . ?"

Inquirers recognize discrepancies and phenomena in their environment and probe into their causes.

Applying Past Knowledge

When confronted with a new and perplexing problem, self-directed learners draw from their past experiences. They can often be heard to say, "This reminds me of . . ." or "This is just like the time when I . . ." They explain what they are doing now in terms of analogies with or references to previous experiences. They call upon their store of knowledge and experience as sources of data to support theories to explain, or processes to solve each new challenge. Furthermore, they are able to abstract meaning from one experience, carry it forth, and apply it in a new and novel situation.

> I've never made a mistake. I've only learned from experience.
>
> —Thomas A. Edison

Too often students begin each new task as if it were being approached for the very first time. Teachers are often dismayed when they invite students to recall how they solved a similar problem previously and students don't remember. It's as if they never heard of it before, even though they had the same type of problem just recently. It is as if each experience is encapsulated and has no relationship to what has come before or what comes afterward. Their thinking is what psychologists refer to as an "episodic grasp of reality" (Feuerstein, Rand, Hoffman, & Miller, 1980). That is, each event in life is a separate and discrete event with no connection to what may have come before or with no relation to what follows. Furthermore, their learning is so encapsulated that they seem unable to draw forth from one event and apply it in another context.

Gathering Data

The brain is the ultimate reductionist. It reduces the world to its elementary parts: photons of light, molecules of smell, sound waves, vibrations of touch—that send electrochemical signals to individual brain cells that store information about lines, movements, colors, smells, and other sensory inputs.

> Observe perpetually.
>
> —Henry James

Self-directed people know that all information gets into the brain through the sensory pathways: gustatory, olfactory, tactile, kinesthetic, auditory, visual. Most linguistic, cultural, and physical learning is derived from the environment by observing or taking in through the senses. To know a wine it must be drunk; to know a role it must be acted; to know a game it must be played; to know a dance it must be moved; to know a goal it must be envisioned. Those whose sensory pathways are open, alert, and acute absorb more information from the environment than those whose pathways are withered, immune, and oblivious to sensory stimuli do.

Furthermore, we are learning more about the impact of arts and music on improved mental functioning. Forming mental images is important in mathematics and engineering; listening to classical music seems to improve spatial reasoning.

Social scientists solve problems through scenarios and role playing; scientists build models; engineers use computer-assisted design/computer-aided manufacturing (CAD/CAM); mechanics learn through hands-on experimentation; artists experiment with colors and textures. Musicians experiment by producing combinations of instrumental and vocal music.

Some students, however, go through school and life oblivious to the textures, rhythms, patterns, sounds, and colors around them. Sometimes children are afraid to touch, get their hands "dirty," or feel some object might be "slimy" or "icky." They operate within a narrow range of sensory problem-solving strategies, wanting only to "describe it but not illustrate or act it," or "listen but not participate."

Imagining, Innovating, and Creating

All human beings have the capacity to generate novel, original, clever, or ingenious products, solutions, and techniques—if that capacity is developed. Creative human beings try to conceive problem solutions differently, examining alternative possibilities from many angles. They tend to project themselves into different roles using analogies, starting with a vision and working backward, imagining they are the objects being considered. Creative people take risks and frequently push the boundaries of their perceived limits (Perkins, 1985). They are intrinsically rather than extrinsically motivated, working on the task because of the aesthetic challenge rather than the material rewards. Creative people are

The vast majority of problems, decisions and situations which confront us daily are those which do not have just one answer. Several solutions are usually possible.

Logic suggests that if one can mentally generate many possible solutions, the more likely it is that an optimum solution will be reached.

This is a creative process—the formation of new and useful relationships.

—Richard E. Manelis

open to criticism. They hold up their products for others to judge and seek feedback in an ever-increasing effort to refine their technique. They are uneasy with the status quo. They constantly strive for greater fluency, elaboration, novelty, parsimony, simplicity, craftsmanship, perfection, beauty, harmony, and balance.

> Creativity can solve almost any problem. The creative act, the defeat of habit by originality, overcomes everything.
>
> —George Lois, Advertising Executive

Students, however, are often heard saying, "I can't draw," "I was never very good at art," "I can't sing a note," "I'm not creative." Some people believe creative humans are just born that way; it's in their genes and chromosomes.

Self-Monitoring

Awareness of Our Own Thinking (Metacognition)

Occurring in the neocortex, metacognition is our ability to know what we know and what we don't know. It is our ability to plan a strategy for producing what information is needed, to be conscious of our own steps and strategies during the act of problem solving, and to reflect on and evaluate the productiveness of our own thinking. While "inner language," thought to be a prerequisite, begins in most children around age five, metacognition is a key attribute of formal thought flowering about age eleven.

> I've reached the moment where the movement of my thoughts interests me more than the thought itself.
>
> —Pablo Picasso

Probably the major components of metacognition are developing a plan of action, maintaining that plan in mind over a period of time, then reflecting back on and evaluating the plan upon its completion. Planning a strategy before embarking on a course of action assists us in keeping track of the steps in the sequence of planned behavior at the conscious awareness level for the duration of the activity. It facilitates making temporal and comparative judgments, assessing the readiness for more or different activities, and monitoring our interpretations, perceptions, decisions, and behaviors. An example of this would be what superior teachers do daily: developing a teaching strategy for a lesson, keeping that strategy in mind throughout the instruction, then reflecting back upon the strategy to evaluate its effectiveness in producing the desired student outcomes.

Self-directed learners plan for, reflect on, and evaluate the quality of their own thinking skills and strategies. Metacognition means becoming increasingly aware of one's actions and the effect of those actions on others and on the environment; forming internal questions as one searches for information and meaning, developing mental maps or plans of action, mentally rehearsing prior to performance, monitoring those plans as they are employed—being conscious of the need for midcourse correction if the plan is not meeting expectations, reflecting on the plan upon completion of the implementation for the purpose of self-evaluation, and editing mental pictures for improved performance.

Persisting

Efficacious people stick to a task until it is completed. They don't give up easily. They are able to analyze a problem, to develop a system, structure, or strategy to attack a problem. They employ a range and have a repertoire of alternative strategies for problem solving. They collect evidence to indicate their problem-solving strategy is working, and if one strategy doesn't work, they know how to back up and try another. They recognize when a theory or idea must be rejected and another employed. They have systematic methods of analyzing a problem, which include knowing how to begin, knowing what steps must be performed, and what data need to be generated or collected. Because they are able to sustain a problem-solving process over time, they are comfortable with ambiguous situations.

> If I had to select one quality, one personal characteristic that I regard as being most highly correlated with success whatever the field, I would pick the trait of persistence. Determination. The will to endure to the end, to get knocked down 70 times and get up off the floor saying, "Here comes number 71!"
>
> —Richard M. Devos, Businessman

Monitoring Clarity and Accuracy

Embodied in the stamina, grace, and elegance of a ballerina or a shoemaker is the desire for craftsmanship, mastery, flawlessness, and economy of energy to produce exceptional results. People who value accuracy, precision, and craftsmanship take time to check over their products. They review the rules

> A man who has committed a mistake and doesn't correct it is committing another mistake.
>
> —Confucius

by which they are to abide; they review the models and visions they are to follow; and they review the criteria they are to employ and confirm that their finished product matches the criteria exactly. To be craftsmanlike means knowing that one can continually perfect one's craft by working to attain the highest possible standards, and will pursue ongoing learning in order to bring a laserlike focus of energies to task accomplishment. These people take pride in their work and have a desire for accuracy as they take time to check over their work. Craftsmanship includes exactness, precision, accuracy, correctness, faithfulness, and fidelity. For some people, craftsmanship requires continuous reworking. Mario Cuomo, a great speechwriter and politician, once said that his speeches were never done—it was only a deadline that made him stop working on them!

Listening to Others With Understanding and Empathy

Highly effective people spend an inordinate amount of time and energy listening (Covey, 1989). Some psychologists believe that the ability to listen to another person, to empathize with, and to understand another's point of view is one of the highest forms of intelligent behavior. Being able to paraphrase other persons' ideas, detecting indicators (cues) of their feelings or emotional states in their oral and body language (empathy), accurately expressing another person's concepts, emotions, and problems—all are indications of listening behavior (Piaget called it "overcoming egocentrism"). They are able to see with the diverse perspectives of others. They gently attend to another person demonstrating, their understanding of and empathy for an idea or feeling by paraphrasing it accurately, building upon it, clarifying it, or giving an example of it.

> Listening is the beginning of understanding . . .
>
> Wisdom is the reward for a lifetime of listening.
>
> Let the wise listen and add to their learning and let the discerning get guidance.
>
> —Proverbs 1:5

Senge and his colleagues (1994) suggest that to listen fully means to pay close attention to what is being said beneath the words. You listen not only to the "music," but also to the essence of the person speaking. You listen not only for what someone knows, but also for what he or she is trying to represent. Ears operate at the speed of sound, which is far slower than the speed of light the eyes take in. Generative listening is the art of developing deeper silences in yourself so you can slow your mind's hearing to your ears' natural speed, and hear beneath the words to their meaning.

While we spend fifty-five percent of our lives listening, it is one of the least taught skills in schools. We often say we are listening, but in actuality we are rehearsing in our head what we are going to say next when our partner is finished. A good listener tries to understand what the other person is saying. In the end he may disagree sharply, but because he disagrees, he wants to know exactly what it is he is disagreeing with.

Self-Modifying

Thinking and Communicating With Clarity and Precision

Language refinement plays a critical role in enhancing a person's cognitive maps and his or her ability to think critically, which is the knowledge base for efficacious action. Enriching the complexity and specificity of language simultaneously produces effective thinking.

> I do not so easily think in words . . . after being hard at work having arrived at results that are perfectly clear . . . I have to translate my thoughts in a language that does not run evenly with them.
>
> —Francis Galton, Geneticist

Language and thinking are closely entwined. Like the two sides of a coin, they are inseparable. Fuzzy language is a reflection of fuzzy thinking. Self-directed people strive to communicate accurately in both written and oral form, taking care to use precise language, defining terms, using correct names and universal labels and analogies. They strive to avoid overgeneralizations, deletions, and distortions. Instead they support their statements with explanations, comparisons, quantification, and evidence.

Responding With Wonderment and Awe

Describing the 200 best and brightest of the All USA College Academic Team identified by *USA Today,* Tracey Wong Briggs (1999) states, "They are creative thinkers who have a passion for what they do." Efficacious people have not only an "I CAN" attitude, but also an "I ENJOY" feeling. They seek problems to solve for themselves and to submit to others. They delight in making up

> The most beautiful experience in the world is the experience of the mysterious.
>
> —Albert Einstein

problems to solve on their own and request enigmas from others. They enjoy figuring things out by themselves, and continue to learn throughout their lifetimes.

Schools must develop learners who are curious, who commune with the world around them, who reflect on the changing formations of a cloud, feel charmed by the opening of a bud, sense the logical simplicity of mathematical order. Self-directed learners find beauty in a sunset, intrigue in the geometrics of a spider web, and exhilaration at the iridescence of a hummingbird's wings. They see the congruity and intricacies in the derivation of a mathematical formula, recognize the orderliness and adroitness of a chemical change, and commune with the serenity of a distant constellation. We want them to feel compelled, enthusiastic, and passionate about learning, inquiring, and mastering.

Continuous Learning

Self-directed people are in a continuous learning mode. Their confidence, in combination with their inquisitiveness, allows them to constantly search for new and better ways. People with these intellectual dispositions are always striving for improvement, always growing, always learning, always modifying and improving themselves. They seize problems, situations, tensions, conflicts, and circumstances as valuable opportunities to learn.

> Wisdom is knowing how little we know.
>
> —Oscar Wilde

A great mystery about humans is that we confront learning opportunities with fear rather than mystery and wonder. We seem to feel better when we know rather than when we learn. We defend our biases, beliefs, and storehouses of knowledge rather than inviting the unknown, the creative, and the inspirational. Being certain and closed gives us comfort while being doubtful and open gives us fear.

From an early age, employing a curriculum of fragmentation, competition, and reactiveness, students are trained to believe that deep learning means figuring out the truth rather than developing capabilities for effective and thoughtful action. They have been taught to value certainty rather than doubt, to give answers rather than to inquire, to know which choice is correct rather than to explore alternatives.

Summary

A goal of education should be to develop creative people who are eager to learn. That includes the humility of knowing that we don't know, which is the highest form of thinking we will ever learn. Paradoxically, unless you start off with humility you will never get anywhere, so as the first step you already have to have what will eventually be the crowning glory of all learning: the humility to know—and admit—that you don't know and are not afraid to find out.

Note

1.   The descriptions of the dispositions in this chapter are extracted from several sources, including Costa and Liebmann (1997b). For a more detailed and expanded list of these dispositions, refer to Costa (2001) and Costa and Kallick (2000a, 2000b, 2000c, 2000d).

CHAPTER 3

Developing the Capacity for Self-Assessment

As many school systems became more explicit about standards, they also became more explicit about defining expectations for how they would expect students to behave as learners. Statements of outcomes, such as the one from Southegan High School in New Hampshire, presented below, serve as a shared vision for the staff, the students, and the community. As such broadly stated outcomes are operationally defined, they become internalized and serve as criteria for students and adults to monitor and govern their own behavior.

> Self-reverence, self-knowledge, self-control.
>
> These three alone lead to sovereign power.
>
> —Lord Tennyson

Academic Learner Expectations

Knowledgeable Person

Acquires and integrates the critical information necessary for success in academic and nonacademic domains

Effectively utilizes the strategies and skills necessary for success in academic and nonacademic domains

Complex Thinker

Effectively translates issues and situations into manageable tasks that have a clear purpose

Effectively uses a variety of complex reasoning strategies

Skilled Information Processor/Consumer

Effectively interprets and synthesizes information

Effectively uses a variety of information-gathering techniques and information resources

Accurately assesses the value of information

Recognizes where and how projects would benefit from additional information

Effective Communicator/Producer

Expresses ideas clearly

Effectively communicates with diverse audiences

Effectively communicates through a variety of mediums

Effectively communicates for a variety of purposes

Creates quality products

Self-Directed Learner

Seeks different perspectives and considers choices before acting

Pushes the limits of his/her ability and perseveres when faced with difficult situations

Establishes clear goals and manages progress toward achieving them

Generates and pursues personal standards of performance

Collaborative Worker

Works toward the achievement of group goals

Demonstrates effective interpersonal skills

Contributes to group maintenance

Self-assesses and monitors own behavior within a group

Responsible Citizen

Shows willingness to work toward improvement of the community

The challenge for a system is to move this set of expectations from rhetoric to reality. As is clear, there is a strong commitment to self-directed learning. In this chapter, we are suggesting that key to self-directed learning is the capacity to become self-assessing. In Chapter 1 we described Marzano's (2001) new taxonomy that includes metacognitive and self-systems. In this chapter we present self-assessment strategies intended to help students become more self-monitoring and to gain greater feelings of self-efficacy. When Marzano refers to the metacognitive system, he identifies four functions: goal specification, process monitoring, monitoring clarity, and monitoring accuracy. When he defines self-system thinking, he refers to four key types: examining importance, examining efficacy, examining emotional response, and examining overall motivation. We will use this system as a means of defining self-assessment. We will detail these systems in light of self-assessment.

Metacognitive Self-Assessment

Self-directed students set goals that are appropriate and attainable. They learn to feel responsible for the work that is to be accomplished. They know the criteria for quality work and know that they are accountable to those criteria. They learn to modify their work based on feedback and self-knowledge.

> Keeping track is a matter of reflective review and summarizing in which there is both discrimination and record of the significant features of a developing experience. It is the heart of intellectual organization and of the disciplined mind.
>
> —John Dewey, *Experience and Education*

Goal Specification, Monitoring Process, Monitoring Clarity, Monitoring Accuracy

These intellectual dispositions of a self-directed learner are fostered in the classroom. Teachers provide time for students to monitor, modify, and manage their work. This work is a part of the instructional focus in the classroom. Following are some classroom examples:

Conferences With Critical Friends

Students meet with an established critical friend. They review the goals that they have set for their work. They follow a protocol so that each partner has time to give and receive feedback. The following steps might serve as a guide.

1. Presenter discusses the goals that he or she has set for accomplishing the work. He discusses his time line and pays attention to whether he is on target for the due date.

2. Responder asks clarifying questions and tries to understand the work plan.

3. Both parties discuss any possible modifications the student might need to make so that he can meet or modify his goals.

4. Partners agree on a time to meet again so that they can check for accuracy and quality.

Conferences With Teachers

Teachers often will have a conference with students that focuses on the time management plan. Students are asked to bring their plan and reflect on where they are at this point in time. Although time-consuming at first, teachers find that this procedure can be shortened once students have an understanding of their responsibility for working in a timely fashion. The conference serves as important instructional time. Some questions that might be asked are,

"What is your work plan?"

"What difficulties are you having in accomplishing your plan?"

"Are your goals realistic given the time frame that you have for accomplishing the work?"

"What are you especially interested in?"

"What strategies have you tried? What strategies might you try?"

"How will you know when your work is ready to turn in?"

A group of elementary teachers developed this set of questions for students in preparation for a conference on goals for the school year:

In Clovis Unified School District, secondary teachers Barbie Hansen and Keith Whelan ask students to lay out a plan of action for

---

WHAT ARE MY GOALS FOR THE YEAR?

My goal concerns myself and my study habits. It is:

_____

_____

_____

A reason I selected this goal is:

_____

_____

_____

The actions I will take to meet this goal are:

_____

_____

_____

Figure 3.1   What Are My Goals for the Year?

the semester. When necessary, they conference with students about this plan. They follow the feedback spiral (see Chapter 1) using the terminology, "Plan, Do, Study, Act."

- **PLAN:** What was your goal for the last six weeks of the grading period? Write it below.
- **DO:** Did you achieve your goal?
- If you did achieve your goal, explain what you did to achieve your goal.
- If you did not achieve your goal, explain why.

- **STUDY:** Look back at what you did during the last six-week grading period. How could you have changed things so that you could improve your performance?
- **ACT:** Set a new goal for the next six weeks.
- **GOAL:** _____

Write down three things that you plan on doing in the coming six weeks to improve your performance and achieve your goals for the last six weeks of the semester.

Recording Progress

Keith Whelan in Clovis Unified School District uses the grid shown in Figure 3.2 for students to fill out. This is a way for students to keep track of their progress toward the class standards.

Students also complete a grade control chart in which they enter the percentage they aim for in a test or in their assignments. They record their targets on a regular basis. They analyze the chart, looking for trends or patterns that can help them gain insight into their learning performance.

Once the students have analyzed their progress, they keep charts that help them identify what the problem might be when they do not meet their target performance.

Self-Reflection Worksheets

Many teachers have designed worksheets for students to fill out one or two times during a period of time when they are in the process of working. For example, Kathleen Reilly uses a series of reflections in her advanced senior seminar. In the second quarter of the year, some of the questions she asks are,

1. When you look through your essays, what particular areas of writing are you struggling with?

2. How are these individual conferences helpful to you? In what ways can I be more helpful to you?

By the last quarter, some of the questions she asks are,

1. Do you have a graphic image of the format of an essay firmly etched in your brain? If so, how does it look? If not, tell me what format you do see.

Name: _____

Class period: _____ Date: _____

Chemistry Standards: Gases and Their Properties

Standard	*Ready for Test	*Need More Practice	*Don't Get It Yet	**Action
Define pressure and explain how it is related to the motion of particles.				
Explain why gases diffuse.				
Apply gas laws to mathematically describe the relationship between temperature, pressure and volume of an ideal gas.				
Define standard temperature and pressure (STP).				
Convert from moles of gas to volume or vice versa at STP.				
Convert from Celsius to Kelvin.				
Explain the meaning of absolute zero.				

*List evidence for your self-rating, quiz score, homework completion, success on review questions, etc.
**What steps will you take to improve your preparedness for the test?

Figure 3.2 (Chemistry Standards)

Name: _____   Period: _____

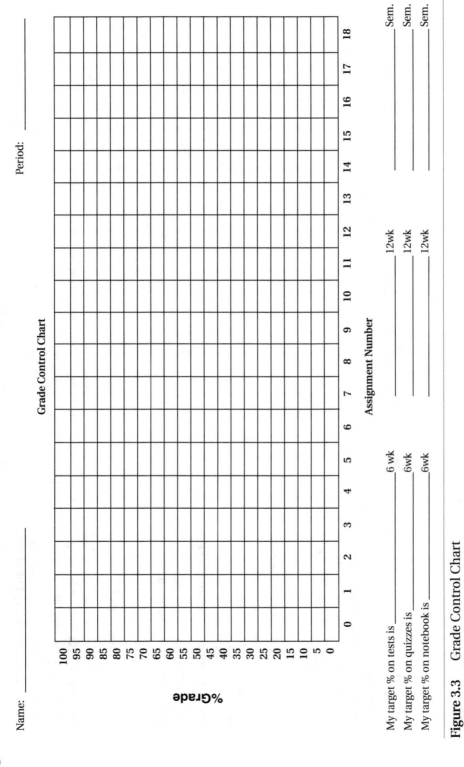

Grade Control Chart

My target % on tests is _____ 6 wk _____ 12 wk _____ Sem.

My target % on quizzes is _____ 6wk _____ 12wk _____ Sem.

My target % on notebook is _____ 6wk _____ 12wk _____ Sem.

Figure 3.3 Grade Control Chart

ASSIGNMENT PROGRESS SHEET   NAME ——————————

PURPOSE: Use this sheet to analyze any assignments that score below your goal. Write in the assignment number, assignment title, and give the reason that you scored below your target grade.

Assignment Number	*Assignment Title*	*Reason this assignment was below my target grade*

Grade Update Information

Date	*Actual points/Total points*	*% Grade*	*Letter Grade*

Figure 3.4   (Assignment Progress Report)

At what specific point within the past forty weeks did you sense that you were actually changing or changed as a writer and thinker about literature? Did you find that you could analyze and support your ideas, reach for insight? If not, what were your frustrations?

2. Please identify your perception of your own strengths as a writer. And then, please follow with your understanding of weaknesses you still have.

3. What else do you need to learn in this course that was not accomplished? What further information would you like me to know?

Another example is a worksheet from *Education by Design* (1998):

1. What were you supposed to do and did you do it?

2. What was your favorite part? Why?

3. What was your least favorite part? Why?

4. How well do you think you understand the key concepts of the challenge?

5. How did you exhibit your understanding?

6. If you could do this task over again, what would you do differently? Why?

7. What rating do you think you deserve? Why?

8. What skills did you work on? How?

9. What goal can you set for yourself for the next challenge?

Glenora Elementary School in Edmonton, Alberta, Canada, has a set of questions that can be adjusted for any subject or age group. All teachers have access to these questions and can draw from them to construct metacognitive reflection sheets. They can be the basis of a worksheet or checklist and can be given at various points in an assignment.

1. Do I understand why I have to read this material? For a test? Report?

2. What do I already know about this subject, topic, issue?

3. Can I make some predictions about this material even before I read it?

4. Do I know where I can get some more information?

5. How much time will I need to learn this?

6. What are some strategies and tactics I can use to learn this?

7. How can I spot an error if I make one?

8. Should I read the first line of a paragraph more than once?

9. Did I understand what I just read?

10. Do I know it well enough to retell it after I finish reading? To answer questions on a test?

Many classroom teachers have searched for ways to make the attributes of self-direction visible and operational to students and observers. As a result, the grids in Figures 3.5 and 3.6 (see below) have become very useful as a way of helping students assess both themselves individually and the groups in which they work.

Teachers can invite students to describe how to determine if the students are becoming more aware of their own thinking (metacognition). They might ask, "How do you think about solving a problem? What steps do you take?"

Teachers might encourage students to do the following:

- List the steps and tell where they are in the sequence of a problem-solving strategy.
- Trace the pathways and dead ends they took on the road to a problem solution.
- Describe what data are lacking and their plans for producing those data.

Or, for persistence: "What would you see a person doing or hear them saying if they are persisting?" Students might say:

- Sticking to it when the solution to a problem is not immediately apparent and you want to give up and quit
- Employing systematic methods of analyzing a problem
- Knowing ways to begin, knowing what steps must be performed, and when they are accurate or are in error
- Taking pride in their efforts
- Self-correcting
- Striving for craftsmanship and accuracy in their products
- Becoming more self-directed in problem-solving abilities

In Clovis Unified School District, secondary teachers Barbie Hansen and Keith Whelan ask the students to fill out these self-reflection questions in addition to the ones that ask about strengths and goals:

1. Who is in charge of your learning?

2. Explain why this person is in charge of your learning.

3. What things can you do as a student to improve your learning ability?

4. Who is responsible for your grade in science? Explain why.

5. Why is focus important in learning?

6. List three things that you can do to focus in class.

Checklists

Checklists may provide an opportunity to experience using, monitoring, and self-evaluating the performance of the standards of performance for the indicators of self-directed learning.

Teachers might ask the question, "What would it look like and sound like if you were persistent?" Or, "What would it look like and sound like if you were aware of your thinking?" Students might generate some of the cues they see when they or members of their group are using these behaviors. Finally, the students and teacher agree to observe these behaviors using a checklist they design together and to reflect on the use of the behaviors upon completion of the task.

Such observations imply self-awareness about one's own and other's skills, styles, and preferences. They require that learners operate from data rather than speculation or hearsay; they are enhanced when students not only contribute ideas, but also know when to relinquish their ideas in favor of others. They mean the ability to clarify and paraphrase. Of most importance, they mean knowing when to silence one's mouth and brain to make room for others' thoughts to be fully entertained (Baker, Costa, & Shalit, 1997; Garmston & Wellman, 1999). A school staff that desires to infuse the dispositions of self-directed learning into their instruction will want to plan for, monitor, and reflect on these dialogical tools in their daily interactions. They will make a conscious effort to improve these skills and seek ways of gathering evidence of their continued growth toward mastery.

Keeping an inventory such as a checklist during class interactions, when solving problems, and after interacting with others can help individuals and groups gather valuable data on which to self-reflect and plan for learning to self-monitor ever more effectively. A class meeting might start with a facilitator drawing from the group and listing criteria or indicators of excellence in meeting management.

Strategic Behavior: Listening With Understanding	Often	Sometimes	Not Yet
Verbal Restates/paraphrases a person's idea before offering personal opinion			
Clarifies a person's ideas, concepts, or terminology			
Expresses empathy for other's feelings/emotions			
Poses questions intended to engage thinking and reflection			
Expresses personal regard and interest			
Nonverbal Faces the person who is speaking			
Establishes eye contact if appropriate			
Nods head			
Uses facial expressions congruent with speaker's emotional message			
Mirrors gestures			
Mirrors posture			
Strategic Behavior: Listening With Empathy	**Often**	**Sometimes**	**Not Yet**
Restates/paraphrases a person's idea before offering personal opinion			
Clarifies a person's ideas, concepts, or terminology			
Expresses empathy for other's feelings/emotions			
Takes an allocentric point of view; e.g., "If I were in your position . . ."			
Changes mind with addition of new information			

Figure 3.5   Listening With Understanding and With Empathy

During a class meeting, students monitor their own, and are aware of each other's, performance. Before the end of the meeting, the teacher asks the students to reflect on the meeting and to describe how the criteria were or were not met. Feelings are explored and indicators of how the team is working more synergistically together are expressed. Teachers may pose such metacognitive questions as,

"What decisions did you make about when and how to participate?"

"What metacognitive strategies did you employ to monitor your own communicative competencies?"

"What were some of the effects of your decisions on you and others in your group?"

"As you anticipate future team meetings, what commitments might you make to strengthen the group's productiveness?"

"What signals in what other future situations will alert you to the need for these communicative competencies?"

See Figures 3.5 and 3.6 for examples of checklists:

Strategic Behavior	Often	Sometimes	Not Yet
Listening with understanding and empathy			
Asking clarifying questions			
Checking on group process			
Distributing tasks equitably			
Checking for accuracy			

Figure 3.6   How Are We Doing: A Process Checklist for Group Work

To begin, the teacher may ask the students to self-assess; for example, "How did I do with the behavior that is representative of openness to learning?" Once students feel comfortable assessing themselves, a

---

WORKING WITH OTHERS

I contribute ideas and information	Not at all _____/	Sometimes _____/	Always _____
I ask for clarification of ideas or more information	Not at all _____/	Sometimes _____/	Always _____
I encourage others to share ideas	Not at all _____/	Sometimes _____/	Always _____
I help keep the group on task	Not at all _____/	Sometimes _____/	Always _____
I explain ideas and processes to others	Not at all _____/	Sometimes _____/	Always _____
I help keep the group organized	Not at all _____/	Sometimes _____/	Always _____

For Next Time:

Figure 3.7   Working With Others

second instruction might be for students to rate themselves as well as the others in their group. Students would then compare ratings and see how accurately they perceive themselves. Finally, the teacher may also rate the students and give specific examples of how students are evidencing the positive behaviors of good listening.

As the students begin to collect data about their behavior over time, they may create a graph of their progress (or lack of it!). They will find it very helpful to receive feedback from their peers, their teacher, and their own assessment of how they are doing.

Another checklist that is used in the Glenora Elementary School in Edmonton, Canada, is shown in Figure 3.7.

Rubrics

Another way of assessing growth toward self-directed learning is to develop scoring rubrics with students. The descriptions for each

> The only person you should ever compete with is yourself. You can't hope for a fairer match.
>
> —Todd Ruthman

scoring category can be developed with students and staff. Each category should be sufficiently clear so that students can learn from the feedback about their behavior and can determine for themselves how to improve.

Rubrics differ from checklists in that they require a quality determination. Checklists ask about frequency or simply whether there is evidence of the behavior or particular criterion in the work. Rubrics require a judgment about the quality of the work. Providing rubrics serves several purposes:

1. They remind students of the teacher's expectations.

2. They provide a systematic way to chart growth and improvement.

3. They provide an explicit language for goal setting and personal mastery.

Vocational Village High School in Portland, Oregon, provides a certificate of employability. Included are four key areas regarding self-directed learning: Work Ethic/Time Management, Problem Solving, Communication, and Teamwork. Their rubric is shown in Figure 3.8.

The rubric can show stages of development. For example, in the rubric on persistence, we have used the language that signifies the development from novice to expert. We have found that students respond to this language favorably. Rather than thinking of themselves as failures, they think of themselves as learners. Everyone is a novice at something. We all suffer the ineptitude of beginning—with a vision of what we would like to be able to do with greater expertise. Most students quickly associate these feelings with athletics. It does not take much prompting for students to remember the first time they rode a bike, tried to roller blade, or played tennis. They have a very concrete vision of what the sport should look like if played well, yet they are stumbling. So it is with the behaviors we consider to be so important for self-directed learning.

Here, for example, is the developmental journey for persistence.

Another way to develop a rubric is through using a scoring procedure. In the rubric below, we have used the range of scores from 4 being the highest to 1 being the lowest. The advantage of this rubric is that students can be more analytical about themselves. They can score high on one criterion and lower on another. This provides an analysis of where they need to focus to improve.

Vocational Village High School
Work-Related Performance Evaluation
Certificate of Employability

Course:	Period:
Teacher:	Credit:
Present:	Absent:	Tardy:

Work Ethic/Time Management	Problem Solving
A. Maintains regular attendance and punctuality	**A. Identifies problems and locates information that may lead to solutions**
☐ 3 (*meeting standard*) 90% attendance and punctuality	☐ 3 (*meeting standard*) Sees problems and checks information sources for the solution
☐ 2 (*in progress*) 75% attendance and punctuality	☐ 2 (*in progress*) Sees problems and goes to the instructor for the solution
☐ 1 (*not meeting standard*) 74% or below attendance and punctuality	☐ 1 (*not meeting standard*) Does not see problems that confront him/her in accomplishing a task
B. Demonstrates accountability for decisions/actions	**B. Identifies alternatives to solve problems, assessing the consequences of the alternatives**
☐ 3 (*meeting standard*) Accepts consequences of actions without blame or complaint, initiates problem-solving steps	☐ 3 (*meeting standard*) Identifies alternatives to solve problems, assessing the consequences of the alternatives
☐ 2 (*in progress*) Accepts consequences of actions without blame or complaint	☐ 2 (*in progress*) Sees multiple possible solutions to a problem but has difficulty selecting the best solution
☐ 1 (*not meeting standard*) Complains or blames others; uncooperative behavior; retaliates	☐ 1 (*not meeting standard*) Sees only one approach to any problem
C. Identifies what needs to be done and initiates actions to complete tasks	**C. Selects and explains a proposed solution and course of action**
☐ 3 (*meeting standard*) Identifies tasks needing to be done and initiates actions to complete tasks	☐ 3 (*meeting standard*) Selects one possible solution to a problem and explains why that solution was chosen
☐ 2 (*in progress*) Asks what needs to be done	☐ 2 (*in progress*) Given a list, picks a reasonable solution but cannot logically support their choice
☐ 1 (*not meeting standard*) Waits to be told what to do	☐ 1 (*not meeting standard*) May not be able to select a logical solution
D. Demonstrates appropriate dress and hygiene for circumstances	**D. Develops a plan to implement the selected course of action**
☐ 3 (*meeting standard*) Displays professional attire appropriate to vocational area or activity	☐ 3 (*meeting standard*) Once a course of action has been selected, can plan the steps and put them in the proper order to best accomplish the task
☐ 2 (*in progress*) Adheres to dress code but does not always choose the most appropriate attire for activity	☐ 2 (*in progress*) Can identify most of the steps to implement a plan but they may not all be in the correct order
☐ 1 (*not meeting standard*) Does not adhere to dress code; detectable body odor or visibly dirty	☐ 1 (*not meeting standard*) Can identify some steps to implement a plan

Comments: _____

Figure 3.8A Work-Related Performance Evaluation

Work-Related Performance Evaluation

Communication	Teamwork
A. Reads technical/instructional materials for information and applies to specific tasks ☐ 3 (*meeting standard*) Reads technical/instructional materials, understanding the information and applying it to specific tasks ☐ 2 (*in progress*) Reads and understands the information but has trouble applying it to a specific situation ☐ 1 (*not meeting standard*) Reads technical/instructional information but does not understand what has been read	**A. Participates as a member of a team** ☐ 3 (*meeting standard*) Works cooperatively with others, delegates tasks, and contributes regularly to group with ideas, suggestions, and effort ☐ 2 (*in progress*) Works cooperatively with others, occasionally contributes ideas and suggestions ☐ 1 (*not meeting standard*) Does not attempt to work cooperatively with others
B. Writes instructions, technical reports, and business communications clearly and accurately ☐ 3 (*meeting standard*) Writes technical reports and business communications clearly and accurately ☐ 2 (*in progress*) Writes written instructions, technical reports, and business communications but they lack clarity and accuracy ☐ 1 (*not meeting standard*) Cannot write instructions of reports that can be understood by others	**B. Exercises leadership; teaches others** ☐ 3 (*meeting standard*) Communicates thoughts, feelings, and ideas. Motivates individuals or groups. Teaches others skills previously mastered ☐ 2 (*in progress*) Participates in leadership roles within the classroom. Teaches others as directed ☐ 1 (*not meeting standard*) Has not demonstrated leadership inside or outside of the classroom
C. Speaks clearly to provide information and directions ☐ 3 (*meeting standard*) Speaks clearly to provide information and directions ☐ 2 (*in progress*) Provides limited information and directions to others verbally ☐ 1 (*not meeting standard*) Cannot provide necessary information to others	**C. Negotiates** ☐ 3 (*meeting standard*) Works toward an agreement that may involve exchanging specific resources or resolving divergent interests ☐ 2 (*in progress*) Supports others who suggest possible ways to resolve divergent interests ☐ 1 (*not meeting standard*) Does not participate in negotiations to resolve differences
D. Listens attentively; gives/receives feedback in a positive manner ☐ 3 (*meeting standard*) Listens attentively and understands instructions. Is able to receive feedback in a positive manner ☐ 2 (*in progress*) Receives most of the information given verbally. Can accept feedback and learn from it ☐ 1 (not *meeting standard*) Unable to concentrate on verbal information; is not able to accept feedback	**D. Works with cultural diversity** ☐ 3 (*meeting standard*) Promotes a cooperative attitude within the classroom, working well with males and females from a wide variety of ethnic, social, and educational backgrounds and encourages others to do so ☐ 2 (*in progress*) Works well with males and females from a wide variety of ethnic, social, and educational backgrounds ☐ 1 (*not meeting standard*) Does not work well with individuals with different backgrounds

Comments: _____

Figure 3.8B   Work-Related Performance Evaluation

	PERSISTENCE
EXPERT	Continues to work no matter how difficult it is to find the answers to solutions. Evaluates the use of a variety of strategies to stay on task.
PRACTITIONER	Continues when trying to find the answers or solutions. Stays on task.
APPRENTICE	Tries to complete tasks when the answers or solutions are not readily available, but gives up when task is too difficult. Gets off task easily.
NOVICE	Gives up easily and quickly on difficult tasks.

Figure 3.9　Rubric for Persistence

Reporting

Self-assessment can be used in relation to report cards. Teachers often have students fill out their report card independently. Then the teacher will conference with the student if there are discrepancies between the way the student sees the work and the way the teacher sees the student's work. The conference provides an excellent means to check for how well the student understands the expectations for learning.

In the Middlefield-Durham, Connecticut, school district they have an elementary report card that includes a focus on social growth and work habits. The criteria they use are:

- Makes appropriate choices to meet work requirements (seat choices, time usage)
- Takes responsibility for own actions
- Follows multi-step directions
- Works cooperatively and productively with a variety of peers
- Makes smooth transitions
- Seeks adult help appropriately when needed (time, manner, relevance)
- Demonstrates care and thoroughness in work
- Makes contribution to school community (study buddy, school chores, school boards, senate, assembly)

Students are given a performance rating for each of these criteria. At the bottom of this report is a set of questions for student response:

Self-Monitoring, Self-Modifying, and Self-Managing

Criteria	4	3	2	1
Sets goals for work	Independently sets work goals that are realistic and appropriate to the task at hand.	Requires reminder to set work goals. Goals are realistic and appropriate to the task at hand.	Requires reminder. Sets work goals that include some unrealistic expectations for the task at hand.	Requires reminder. Sets minimal goals that indicate minimal expectations for the task at hand.
Monitors progress toward goals	Independently revises and adjusts time-management plans throughout work process.	Requires reminders to make adjustments to work process.	Requires continual reminders to maintain a well-balanced work process.	Requires frequent reminders and shows evidence of poor time management.
Monitors for clarity and under-standing	Independently revises work for depth of meaning. Solicits outside readers to confirm clarity of communication.	Requires suggestion to revise work. Responds to suggestion for outside reader to confirm clarity of communication.	Requires continual reminders to revise work and check for understanding.	Requires frequent reminders and resists revision and feedback for clarity and meaning.
Monitors for accuracy	Independently checks for accuracy.	Requires suggestion to check for accuracy.	Requires continual reminder to check for accuracy.	Requires frequent reminders and resists checking for accuracy.

Figure 3.10   Rubric for Metacognition

1. What goals are you meeting? How do you know?

2. What goals do you still need to meet? How do you know?

3. What will you do to improve by the next marking period?

In the primary school in Somers, New York, Julie Gherardi asks her second-grade students to fill out a report card she calls "How I Think I'm Doing in Second Grade." Figure 3.11 shows an excerpt from a student's report card.

At Glenora Elementary School, upper-grade students assess their capabilities in working with others using the form shown in Figure 3.7 (see page 47).

Students write their own progress reports. Students are given an assignment to complete a progress report in which they are to:

Give specific and detailed strengths and areas for growth. Use full sentences. For the areas for growth, suggest a strategy that you could use to improve your skills and abilities in this area. For example, if an area for growth for you is spelling, write "_____ needs to improve his or her spelling by using a dictionary at all times." Or, if an area for growth is writing in full sentences, write "_____ needs to improve his or her ability to write in full sentences by proofreading his or her work. He or she can read work out loud, and think, 'Is this really a sentence?'"

Barbie Hansen, in Clovis Unified School District, asks the students to provide their parents with a progress report. Since they are keeping track of their performance in the class in their own folders, they can explain their grade to their parents far better than the teacher can. See Figure 3.12 for an example of a six-week progress and grade update (on page 55).

Self-System Thinking: Importance, Efficacy, Emotional Response, and Motivation

Interviews

Conducting interviews with students can enlighten the student and the teacher at the same time. For example, in Glenora Elementary School, the teacher asks what the students know about themselves as readers. The answers to these questions help individual students become aware of how they think about reading and, at the same time, might provide insights into ways the teacher can help each student

Working With Others - (Circle the phrases that most describe you and then describe yourself in your own words.)

I can follow directions after just hearing them once.

It takes me a long time to follow directions - sometimes I don't hear them the first time.

I work quietly - so I don't bother anyone around me.

I like to talk a lot - sometimes it keeps me or my teammates from getting things done.

I can wait patiently.

I hate to wait - so sometimes I just interrupt or yell out.

I am kind to others most of the time - I never want to hurt anyone's feelings.

Sometimes I bother other kids because it makes me look cool.

I work hard to make my class the best it can be.

I think it's the teacher's job to make the class terrific.

I work well in a team - I can listen to others and add my own ideas, too.

I would rather work alone - I don't like to listen to others and I would rather keep my own ideas to myself.

I love working a planing I be find to others

Thinking and Working - (Circle the phrases that most describe you and then describe yourself in your own words.)

I always do my homework on time.

I only do my homework if my parents remind me to do it.

I keep my work space neat - I always know where all my things are

I lose things all the time - I can't keep my work space neat.

I have lots of good ideas - I like to think about the things we're doing in class

I usually don't concentrate too much on what we're doing - sometimes I'm thinking about other things.

I do my best as a second grader

I do things because I have to.

I am a good liginer and I do my homwork

Figure 3.11   Student Self-Evaluation: Working With Others

6 WEEK PROGRESS AND GRADE UPDATE
Mrs. Hansen's Science Class

Name _____
Period _____
Date _____

Grading period: 1st Semester grade report
PARENTS: FRIDAY JANUARY 18TH IS THE END OF THE 1ST SEMESTER
GRADING PERIOD. ALL LATE WORK OR MISSING ASSIGNMENTS MUST BE
IN BY THURSDAY, JANUARY 17TH.
THERE ARE 2 WEEKS LEFT IN THE 1ST SEMESTER!
Current grade:
My Total points _____   Class Points Possible _____
% Grade _____   Letter Grade _____

Number of missing assignments_____
List the titles of missing assignments below:

Student explanation of current grade:

Parents please respond to grade explanation and current grade, write
comments or concerns:

Student goal for the next 6-week grading period:

Parent response: I plan to help my child achieve this goal by:

Student signature _____   Date _____

Parent signature _____   Date _____

Figure 3.12   Six-Week Progress and Grade Update

become more strategic as a reader. The following is an excerpt from an interview:

Q. "What did you learn about yourself as a reader?"

A. "I am a speed reader. I read in my head."

Q. "Do you read word by word or do you see a whole section at a time?"

A. "I read complete thoughts at a time."

"I discovered that I read the same thing over and over and then I realize I haven't really been reading."

Q. "Can you think of a strategy to help with this problem?"

A. "Point with my finger."

"Uncover with a book mark."

"I read slow, but I understand what I read. I don't use my voice, but I move my lips. If I don't move my lips I can read faster in my head but I don't understand what I read."

Q. "Do you eventually want to read in your head?"

A. "Yes."

Fred Newman, of the University of Wisconsin, includes this interview in his work:

TESTING PROCEDURE

1. Read the question to me. If you don't know a word, leave it out. (To identify reading errors)
2. Tell me what the question is asking you to do. (To identify errors in comprehension)
3. Tell me how you are going to find the answer. (To identify transformation errors)
4. Show me what to do to get the answer. Tell me what you are doing as you work. (To identify errors in the use of process skills)
5. Now write down the answer to the question. (To identify encoding errors)

Checklists

Students develop a sense of efficacy from knowing when they have met the standards that define quality work. Although there is much conversation about standards in schools, Pekin, Illinois, decided to help students make regular determinations about whether they perceived themselves as meeting the standards. They translated the state standards into "kid-friendly" language and provided a checklist for self-assessment. See Figure 3.13 for an excerpt from sixth-grade Language Arts (on page 58).

Questionnaires

Many teachers ask a set of self-reflective questions such as,

"What am I good at doing that I want to improve?"

"What would help me get better at _____?"

"What do I need to work on?"

"What am I especially interested in?"

"What do I avoid trying and what will help me to begin to work at it?"

Once students are engaged in answering these questions, teachers conference with students to set up a work plan for growth.

In Crow Island School in Winnetka (Illinois) Public Schools, a reflective questionnaire accompanies each portfolio. The qualities teachers and students focus on are: self-confidence, self-control, communication, cooperation, and relating to others. They believe that these qualities support the student as a learner in their learning community. Questionnaires are sent to parents as well as provided for students. Figure 3.14 is an excerpt from a parent's reflections:

Following is an excerpt from this parent's fourth-grade child's reflection on the same set of questions (Author's Note: *Corrections have been made to student spelling.*):

PERSEVERANCE: Can you stick to a difficult task and get it done? Give examples of when you know you needed to spend more time on a task. Give examples of when you were willing to put forth more effort on a difficult task.

PEKIN PUBLIC SCHOOLS DISTRICT 108

I Can Do It!

| STUDENT NAME | + = YES |
| TEACHER NAME | ✓ = NOT YET |

READING

	FALL		WINTER		SPRING	
	S	T	S	T	S	T

Read and understand text using strategies I know.

Preview the material I will be reading and predict what I need to know.

Check and explain my predictions using information from a story.

Find useful information quickly in non-fiction sources.

Read aloud accurately and with expression.

Find the main idea in the selection i read.

Compare and contrast a variety of reading selections

Summarize what I read and apply it to real life.

Make inferences, draw conclusions, and compare experiences when reading.

Relate the characters, settings and plots of literature I read to current and historical events people and different points of view.

Identify different types of text.

Explain how an author shows his point of view

Identify and explain themes from different types of literature.

WRITING

	FALL		WINTER		SPRING	
	S	T	S	T	S	T

Write narrative, expository and persuasive paragraphs that include a variety of sentence types with appropriate use of parts of speech, capitalization, punctuation and correct spelling.

Plan and organize my ideas before I begin to write.

Add details to my planned topic so that the reader will understand my ideas.

Edit my writing.

Share my ideas using a variety of media and technologies.

6th Grade Language Arts

Figure 3.13 "I Can Do It" Checklist

THE WINNETKA PUBLIC SCHOOLS
FALL PARENT REFLECTION
FOURTH GRADE

Student: _____   Teacher: _____

In the Winnetka Public Schools, we place the highest priority on knowing your child. Your child brings a unique way of approaching learning, people and life to our school community. Therefore, we highly value your input. Please take time to write about your child's strengths and needs in as many of the following areas as possible.

Self-confidence:
Describe how your child approaches new tasks and situations. *"I CAN'T DO THAT" IS HEARD MOST FREQUENTLY ABOUT MATH. IN OTHER REALMS, JOHN IS OFTEN INITIALLY EXCITED, THEN INSTANTLY ANGRY & FRUSTRATED WHEN SOMETHING REQUIRES MORE CAREFUL EFFORT TO WORK OR LOOK THE WAY HE ENVISIONS. I WAS DELIGHTED WHEN JOHN ENJOYED SKI SCHOOL. I WAS WORRIED HE MIGHT SIT OUT MOPING.*

Curiosity:
Describe areas in which your child exhibits interest. (Ex. sports, science, arts, etc.) *JOHN PRIDES HIM*
How does he/she pursue them? *ON KNOWING INTRIGUING SCIENCE & NATURE FACTS. HE SETS UP KITCHEN SINK EXPERIMENTS. ENJOYS WORKING WITH TOOLS. HE BUILDS & PAINTS SIMPLE THINGS. I KNOW HE ENJOYS ART AT SCHOOL, AND HE IS REALLY "INTO" MUSIC - PLAYING HIS CDS OVER & OVER NOODLING ON HIS CELLO & RECORDER. WITH FRIENDS THEY SOMETIMES PLAY ALONG TO MUSIC ON ELECTRONIC DRUMS & KEYBOARDS LIKE A BAND. JOHN ISN'T TOO INTERESTED IN SPORTS, LIKES HIS SCOOTER & HAS PICKED UP ON THE TONY HAWKS PRO RAGER FAD, BUT DOESN'T PURSUE IT ACTIVELY HIMSELF. JOHN LOVES ARMY MOVIES, PARAGONS, KNIVES ETC.*

Self-control:
Describe your child's ability to monitor his or her behavior and act appropriately in different situations. *JOHN'S SELF CONTROL AT OTHER PEOPLE'S HOMES & AT SCHOOL, SEEMS FINE. AT HOME HE BLOWS OFF A LOT OF STEAM. I HAVE A REAL PROBLEM WITH HIM SWEARING & TALKING RUDELY IN FRONT OF HIS LITTLE SISTER.*

Communication:
Describe how your child communicates ideas, feelings, or concepts with others, including adults, in one-on-one or group situations. *JOHN IS SENSITIVE & EXPRESSES THOUGHTS & FEELING VERY WELL. HE CAN COMMUNICATE COMPLEX IDEAS & CONCEPTS CLEARLY. HE & HIS FRIENDS ACTUALLY SPEND A FAIR AMOUNT OF TIME TALKING, AND HE SOMETIMES WANTS TO TALK THINGS OVER WITH ME.*

Figure 3.14   Parent Reflection (Winnetka, Illinois)

Student Response: "Yes, I have used my perseverance. When I was doing long division. It was very long and hard but I did it. I still want to improve for the future when I'm in high school."

SELF-CONFIDENCE: Compared to earlier this year, do you feel more confident when you approach new work or play situations?

Student Response: "Yes because I've had more experience. Now I can speak my mind thanks to my teacher and all the hard work. I liked some of the tasks that's what kept me going all year! But I also wanted to give up and strop trying all together!"

SELF-CONTROL: In what ways have you seen changes in your ability to control your reactions to things you don't like? In what ways have you seen changes in your ability to behave well when adults are not watching?

Student Response: "Yes. Now I have some more self-control. When I'm mad I can just bite my lip. Now I've learned how to cope with new work. I just think I'm able and that I'm knowledgeable and I can also get help from my teacher and my parents."

Communication/Cooperation: Compared to earlier in the year, are you better able to communicate your ideas and feelings? Do you work well and show respect for others in teamwork? Give examples that describe your ability to communicate ideas and feelings. Give examples that describe your cooperation.

Student Response: "I try to tell when my view or the other way that I think it should be. But some times all I get is lip and the wrong way to do it. Though I'm not always right, I try to communicate and cooperate."

RELATING TO OTHERS: Give examples of good relationships with others at home or at school.

Student Response: "With my friends when someone is feeling bad we try to cheer them up. Then we all play tag or something."

Give examples of difficult relationship with others at home or at school.

Student Response: "Sometimes when someone gets tagged they partner up and one untags and then one tags."

CURIOSITY: In what ways have you followed your interest and talents this year in schoolwork as well as activities outside the school?

Student Response: "I'm curious about different writing like gliphs and Russian. Maybe even taking a class when I get older. I think it would be fun to speak Spanish, English and Russian!"

COMMUNICATION: Do you feel you are able to find the words you need to communicate your ideas and feelings in speaking and writing tasks? Give examples and describe your ability to express yourself.

Student Response: "No. I'm too shy sometimes and then I think all my work is poorly done. But my work is really not that poor like when I write. So I want to improve on my communication skills."

RESPONSIBILITY: Describe ways you have shown responsibility for assignments and projects in your fourth-grade studies. At what times have you asked for help when you needed it?

Student Response: "I've shown responsibility in my assignments by trying to do them early. But I usually don't get them complete until the last minute. I want to improve on my responsibility."

Letters

Sometimes writing a letter to a particular audience helps students become aware of their thinking. As they formalize their perceptions about how they are working, they are able to become more personal. They often find it easier to address someone and recount their interests and how they feel they are particularly skillful. These letters serve as an early experience for writing résumés for the workplace or for college applications.

Nadine McDermott in Irvington Public Schools in New York asks students to write a friendly letter to their parents summarizing their accomplishments in her music class. She asks them to discuss the activities that they found enjoyable and/or valuable. Some thought starters she provides follow:

- Here is my work
- This is how I approached it
- These are the habits of mind I used
- This is why I value _____
- This is how I evaluate _____
- This is how my teachers evaluated _____
- This is how I have changed
- This is what I need to work on next

Many teachers require students to write a letter to next year's teacher. In that letter students have the opportunity to tell the teacher about themselves as learners. For example:

There are things to celebrate about having me in your classroom.

I am good at

_____

_____

_____

There are things that I might need help with in your classroom. I have difficulty with

_____

_____

_____

What really makes me feel excited about learning is

_____

_____

_____

Linda Bachta, in her seventh-grade science class in Winnetka, Illinois, asks her students to write a letter to the reader of their portfolios answering these questions: What am I learning? How am I learning? Why am I learning? Who am I becoming? One student wrote:

Dear whoever may be viewing my portfolio,

In the first seventh grade trimester with Mrs. Bacta, I have had a blast! I have learned so many new facts of life and I look forward to learning a ton more. There are so many things to mention abut what we learned, so I will start with a broad topic called Microbiology. In our unit of microbiology we used the microscope so much I actually got bored of it. Throughout the unit we learned about what the cells of different organism look like and some odds and ends under the

Figure 3.15 *(Continued)*

(Continued)

microscope. For example, hair, thread, newspaper, onion root cells dead cork cells, elodea leaf cells, cheek skin cells, yogurt, fish embryo cells, bone of a human, muscle of a human, blood of a human, fat of a human, skin of a human, protozoans, and pond water. We also learned about how to do really good research and present very well in our famous person project. Not only did we get to see what different cells look like, but we learned their functions, how they reproduce, AND the organelles inside of them. Along with those many things, we also learned about photosynthesis and respiration, the way that organisms make their own food. That wasn't one of the high points since I also learned about that last year. One of the most exciting things I think I did was the egg lab. In this lab we learned about how osmosis and diffusion work. The experiment really got my attention of not wanting to eat eggs ever again!

When I learn it was to be fun and interesting, not just sitting in my seat listening to the teacher talk. That gets me so bored and it really makes me dislike school, which I don't like to happen, but unfortunately that is one of the main ways that kids learn. Luck for me Mrs. Bacta's class is a very interactive and fun class, well that is compare to my last teacher. We watch videos, take notes, read the textbook, conduct labs (my favorite, build models, use the microscope, do oral presentations, have demonstrations, do internet research, make drawings and diagrams, play games, have discussions, and make observations. I think that my most favorite and the best way that I learn is by conducting labs and building models. I think that is because I am a more active person and can't really sit still, therefor my doing labs I can move around. Another reason is because I don't always understand things when I just read it from a textbook; I have to see it done. My least favorite and the more difficult way for me to learn is by reading the textbook that's because I read it to fast and the I don't get it, because it is so boring to read it. I hope that some day there will be many new ways to read and better textbooks that you can understand more!

The future of my life is what I look forward to most, but I have to get there by passing where I am now. To pass where I am now, I have to learn, have fun, and enjoy my life. Part of why I learn is to get and have a good career that I enjoy. I think that the science that I ma learning won't really get me to the career of being a dancer, actress, or singer. Although it could get me to have a business job, to earn money for personal needs. I also want to learn for personal goals, such as

Figure 3.15 *(Continued)*

(Continued)

going to college, or someday being as smart as my brother. Its also nice to just know things about science. They may help me be aware of my body and my health. Science may also help me talk intelligently to my doctor about how I am feeling and about how maybe I could cure the sickness. I don't find that I enjoy science a ton, and I don't see much of it in my future but then again, you never know.

The learning of my everyday life used to seem as if it was a punishment. I used to hate going to school and learning every day, but now I realize why I do go to school. I think it is because it is guiding me to who I am becoming, the one and only me. My learning of science affects me a person, because it changes my awareness. As I learn I see how delicate the human body is, and the environment around us. If I didn't learn science I wouldn't care what could harm my insides, such as smoking, or drinking. I wouldn't care if I saw people cutting down trees, or if they were throwing garbage everywhere. I just wouldn't be the same because I wouldn't be as caring towards the environment. My learning affects myself as a family member a whole lot. My family is very caring of the earth, especially the ocean. If I didn't learn all of the science I am learning, I would have no idea of why my brother wants to become a marine biologist. I would really like to work towards being aware of what I do. I don't want to walk down the sidewalk and tear leaves off the trees, or kick the grass around. I want to just walk and not harm anything around me. I want to be the best that I can possibly be.

From L. B.

Figure 3.15   Student Letter to Reader of Portfolio

Portfolios

Portfolios can tell us who we are and who we want to be. They can help us continuously recreate the narrative of our own learning. Powerful classrooms help students arrive at an understanding of themselves through collecting work over time that they can reflect back on. All of the failures and misfires are in a portfolio, but they are next to the triumphs and breakthroughs! Peers cheer the growth they see, the power of words selected, the essays they wish they had written. Students delight in their changes, cherish the praise, and work even harder to produce an admirable product. Beyond the chronological history of producing work, being evaluated, and working toward improving, there is the deeper layer where the patterns of their work tell a personal story of where they are at this time. This is an ideal opportunity for students to provide evidence and reflect on what makes them feel efficacious, what engages them, and how they view themselves as learners. Everyone hands in a paper, for sure; the process of creating it is greatly enhanced by careful and deliberate attention to the choices that moved them. They begin to see, through their performances, the way the intellectual dispositions affect their writing. They review their performances, asking whether they persisted in the face of uncertainty, used precise language, showed wonderment and curiosity, checked for accuracy.

By the end of the year, students can show where they have grown and they can articulate the reasons for their improvement. This is a meaningful assessment because it holds the promise that they will continue to collect and assess their work well after they leave the classroom.

A portfolio is a collection of work, developed over time, with an accompanying reflection to show why that work was chosen for the portfolio. There are many formats that teachers use for the reflection that accompanies the work. The following are some examples:

The process I went through to create this piece

Who or what influenced me to create this piece

Risks I took in the creation of this piece

New insights I gained about myself as I created this piece

This piece was an experiment for me because _____

I have discovered that I am good at _____

What continues to intrigue me is _____

The evidence that I have that shows my growth is _____
_____

The portfolio can be sectioned with folders, each with an attribute of self-directed learning as a heading (e.g., Persisting, Monitoring for Accuracy, Innovating, Creating, etc.). Students choose work based on their best example of when they were persistent in their work, or when they felt that their work reflected their flexibility. The work is entered in the portfolio and the student reflects on why that work has been chosen and what it should say to the reader of the portfolio. Students coach one another as they build these portfolios by having peer conferences. One teacher asks the students to read the work in the portfolio and help the learner reflect on why he or she has chosen

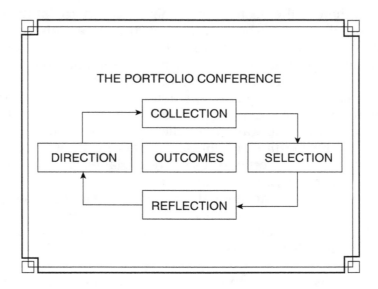

Figure 3.16   Portfolio Conference

particular pieces. When portfolios are developed around self-directed learning, they are transdisciplinary—one portfolio can include artifacts from all subjects. This is an especially useful design for high school students.

A high school student writes a reflection on his writing portfolio, a carefully selected body of work that represents his growth as a learner. The following is an excerpt:

> If a stranger opened my portfolio, this is what he would see: four descriptive exercises, two poems, a book review, an essay, a journal entry, a letter, a parody, and a short story. I, however, see the explorations of a writer.
>
> . . . I was told to write a talk of my own, using Chaucer's style. . . . While writing it, I realized how difficult it must have been for Chaucer to create elaborate stories that rhyme. It was very time consuming to rearrange sentences and add words here and there in order to make the lines rhyme. After three drafts, I have finally rid my poem of "stupid" rhymes. I am now pleased with the story—particularly with the ironic ending.

Or, for example, the teacher in a high school science class gave this prompt for students to respond to when entering a piece of writing in the portfolio:

Explain how you decided what to revise and improve in this entry. Be specific about what you learned that led you to make the revisions.

One student's response:

I wrote the first draft of this paper before we started studying the periodic table, so it didn't have much information. It was mainly a collection of random facts I had picked up in earlier science classes, such as the fact that the atomic number of an element referred to how many protons it had, or the fact that the noble gases all give off a different color neon light. My first draft didn't have a real thesis or point.

My second draft was written three months later, and was definitely more cohesive. I gave a history of the periodic table and explained how the modern table is helpful to students who have trouble memorizing the charges on ions. But I still didn't have a thesis, and my essay was very general. My mom read it and said that I should give examples for each trend I talked about, instead of just listing trends.

So I wrote my third draft, which was a very long explanation of several different periodic trends. I talked about electron configurations, atomic radii, ionization energy, electron affinity, and electronegativity. I gave it to my dad to read because he loves science. He asked me what was the point I was trying to make. I looked at my essay and realized I wasn't making any point: I was just explaining. I asked him what the thesis should be, and he said, "I'll give you one clue. What does the atomic number mean?"

I thought about that for a long time. I knew that the trends occurred when the elements were placed in order of atomic number, but why? What does atomic number mean? Finally I got it. Atomic number means how many protons and how many electrons are in an atom. This is the key to all of the periodic trends! They all depend on how many protons and how many electrons are in an atom. There was my thesis.

I wrote my final draft with that in mind. I didn't explain all of the periodic trends; I just picked one physical trend and one chemical trend and explained why those worked in terms of numbers of protons and electrons. My new essay had a thesis, it made a point, it was shorter, and it all fit together. Finally!

From an elementary class in Glenora Elementary School, a student writes about what he thinks about a piece of work:

What inspired me to do my piece was when I was looking with my view finder I really liked all the interesting bones in the foot. At first I just drew the whole foot. Well, right away everybody knew that it was a boney foot. But, I still liked the bones in the foot. I decided to get a view closer up. I really liked all the little bones in between the toes and the heel because of all the interesting shapes. That's what I drew.

Summary

We must make our good intentions a reality. It is insufficient to merely name our expectations through a vision or set of learner expectations. We must make certain that what we name, we explicitly instruct and assess. Students need the opportunity to look back at their work. Too often, we hear students say, "I already finished that work. What more do you want?" When teachers focus on self-assessment, the question is reversed. It is, "What more do *I* want?" Striving for excellence is a life task, not a singular event to satisfy a teacher. We want to see students develop a love of learning and not depend solely on the judgment of others to determine the value of what they are learning. The many examples provided in Chapters 3 and 4 offer possibilities. Teachers provide opportunities. Given those opportunities, students continuously assess themselves and build the strength and humility of continuous learning. As one student reflects about herself: "I don't care what other people say. I love it and I don't think it will change. I participate and get along with people. So I'm just fine the way I am."

CHAPTER 4

Assessing the Conditions for Self-Directed Learning

W hile each of us is responsible for the spirit in our own lives, teachers of children and administrators of schools have the positional power to create conditions that will give others greater opportunity to develop self-directedness. Instead of demanding conformity and compliance, they assume a new role in mediating and supporting others to become more self-reliant, self-accountable, and self-referencing. It is easier to be and to teach others to be self-directed when the organization supports

> To care for another person, in the most significant sense, is to help him grow and actualize himself.
>
> —Milton Mayeroff,
> *On Caring*

these efforts. Students and staff can grow, create, and contribute without having to struggle every step of the way or without subverting their innate drive to become self-assertive and innovative.

In this chapter we provide many examples from school systems and schools of how they promote self-directed learning. We offer assessment strategies so that school administrators and teachers may assess the degree to which self-directed learning is being manifested in their school and classroom cultures.

Infusing Self-Directed Learning in Goals, Outcomes, and Intentions

There is a greater likelihood that teachers will teach for and students will learn the values of self-directed learning if those ideals are apparent in the school's curriculum and its culture. Teachers will adopt visions of self-directed learning for their own students and will value exacting standards, flexibility, cooperation, and creativity in thoughtful, interdependent environments.

> One of the sources of pride in being a human being is the ability to bear present frustrations in the interests of longer purposes.
>
> —Helen Merrell Lynd

Because some students may have come from homes or from other schools where self-directed learning was not valued, they may be dismayed by and resistant to the teacher's invitations to plan for themselves, monitor themselves, and reflect on and derive meaning from their own experiences. School staffs, therefore, must clearly convey to parents and students that their goal of education is self-directed learning, including these ideals:

- Thinking is the student's responsibility.
- Having more than one solution is desirable.
- Taking time to plan and reflect on multiple possible answers is more commendable than responding rapidly or impulsively.
- Changing an answer in the light of additional information is more desirable than holding fast to an initial answer.

These values can be clearly communicated throughout the school's mission statements, standards, outcomes, reports to parents, student handbooks, orientation materials, and newsletters.

For example, Encinal High School in Alameda, California, composed and adopted the following mission statement. While this mission statement does not use the same terminology that we might use, the thoughts clearly are congruent with the ideals of self-directed learning:

> Encinal High School is a home for the active mind—a cooperative community promoting knowledge, self-understanding, mutual respect, global understanding, adaptability to change, and a love for lifelong learning.

Leadership: Building a Self-Directed Community for Learning

Some administrators assume the position in which they feel powerful when they dispense advice, make demands, and solve other's problems. Yet teachers and students continually struggle to assert their own voice and direction in encounters with those who exert authority over them.

> If you want to manage somebody, manage yourself. Do that well and you'll be ready to stop managing and start leading.
>
> —Anonymous

To build other's autonomy and authenticity, leaders must transcend their "superior/inferior" relationships (Lambert, 2003; Lambert et al., 2002). It is easy to find teachers and students who feel like vassals, but it is harder to find active learners who are their own masters. Almost all of us can envision the orderly classroom where the concerned and well-meaning teacher, through the cunning use of rewards and punishments, turns self-asserting, self-fulfilling children into compliant learners. We are suggesting that we hold a vision of a classroom in which students are working with interdependence, thoughtfully pursuing their work at their own pace, making choices about how and what they are learning—all achieved through a well-structured environment that provides the appropriate boundaries for self-directed learning. Interestingly enough, we are more likely to see such an environment in a primary classroom than we are in a secondary classroom.

Administrator and teacher must shift their mental maps from, "How can I motivate others?" to, "How can I create the condition in which *they* will motivate themselves?" (Deci, 1995).

If you believe that knowledge comes from a single authoritative source, then discussion, problem solving, and critical analysis have little pertinence. The body of knowledge is fixed and needs only to be transmitted to the learner. But if you believe that knowledge is constructed socially, that it is the collective understanding of people at a given point in time, then the learning environment needs to be a place in which learners engage in the examination of knowledge as a regular habit. It needs to be a place where collectively the goal is to inquire about how you know what you know—as well as how you can better inform what you know through active engagement with one another, with media (curriculum, text, film), with those outside of your immediate environment, with your own observations. It needs to be a place of interdependent learners. Participation in a self-directed learning community requires a climate of trust and a sense of safety. The natural dilemmas raise questions in one's mind:

1. Is there really a "right" answer or am I actually being asked to think "outside the box"?

2. How will I be evaluated fairly? Are the criteria going to be apparent or will there be inexplicit expectations?

3. Will judgments be made about me based on my race, my class, or my gender that may preclude my thinking from being acceptable or will the group welcome diversity?

4. If my ideas are not well received, will that affect my relationships with members of the group?

5. Dare I express the negative? The dark side of the picture? Does the group allow for acceptance of the gloomy? The critical negative judgment?

6. Will I get my chance to talk if I listen or will everything start to build on someone else's ideas and my idea will never get a chance to surface?

7. How can I trust my actions, my decisions? Is there nothing that I can hold on to as certain?

Teachers and administrators create conditions that bring forth potential for themselves and others. They create these conditions because they want to have better results on behalf of student learning. In addition, they want to contribute to the larger evolution of humanity necessary for a sustainable world. They create these conditions because they care.

Caring teachers and administrators respond to the needs of others and enable and trust others to grow on their own time and own way. They encourage people to be themselves, let them make their own decisions, and help people achieve what they want.

They loosen boundaries, encourage dialogue, and build trust. They share information—including bad news. They talk about loss, failure, and disappointment and learn from these little deaths. They refrain from using bribes and threats in futile efforts to control and motivate teachers and students.

They expect leadership at all levels. They see staff development as an opportunity for self-determination. They do not "fix" people. Rather, they set clear expectations that allow people to design their work in ways that enhance their capabilities. They hold people accountable for developing the capacities that will enhance student learning. They do not fear confronting mediocrity. They are guided by a sense of the power of continuously learning and improving.

Using Protocols

Every learner is a leader—a person who can facilitate the learning in others. However, it is often helpful to use a protocol to guide discussions in order to make certain that the discussion remains focused.

Often these protocols are used at department meetings, grade level meetings, or faculty meetings. The real power of the protocol is that it provides a safe place for collaboration around practices. Teachers are not accustomed to making their practices public. Much of what happens in the classroom is rarely examined by anyone other than the teacher. Private thoughts about success or failure, or concerns about teaching and learning are often covered over by sharing handouts or resources. When teachers actually look at student work and the practices that brought the students to the quality of work that they produced, they are entering unfamiliar territory. A protocol provides time and structure for such conversations.

At Glenora School in Edmonton, Alberta, Canada, Mary Michailides, the principal, invites teachers to examine how they are looking at student's work.

Looking at Student Work Collaboratively

"How it can work!"

Self-Reflection

When looking for evidence of student thinking:

- Stay focused on the evidence that is present in the work.
- Avoid judging what you see initially.
- Look openly and broadly, don't let your expectation cloud your vision.
- Look for patterns in the evidence that provide clues to *how* and *what* the student was thinking.

Essential questions for looking at student work

1. Why did I collect this sample of work?

2. Define the objectives of the lesson.

3. How was this information shared with the students?

4. What criteria did students use to evaluate this work?

5. What learning did I acquire from this activity?

6. How could/did I modify my teaching practices after this lesson?

(*Continued*)

(Continued)

    7._____

    8._____

    9._____

Celebration of Successes

    10._____

    11._____

    12._____

Other Feedback

    13._____

    14._____

Self-Directed Learning Throughout the System

Angus McBeath, Superintendent of the Edmonton Public Schools in Alberta, Canada, promotes self-directed learning throughout the entire school system. He states,

> In Edmonton Public Schools, we would define self-directed learning as distributed leadership and effective decision making by staff. Both of these have been fostered by our district over a number of decades and in different ways. More than two decades ago, we implemented site-based decision making which has enabled principals and school staffs to make key decisions about the teaching and learning that is occurring in their schools. In addition, we have implemented a range of programs of choice over the past two decades in order to enable schools to create a program that is responsive to the needs of their students and parents, such as second language programs and programs with a focus on a particular pedagogy. Lastly, in Central Services, we have offered a range of professional development programs from which schools can choose. Participation in these programs is determined by the principal and school staff and is offered on a cost-recovery basis. As a result, we have an extensive history in the district of supporting and building individual and school choice and expertise.

A District Perspective

Following is a message from principals about the leadership in Edmonton Public Schools. It should be obvious that the Superintendent values self-directed learning throughout his district.

Principals believe the following makes a difference in their schools!

—(Written by Mary Michailides,
Principal, Glenora School)

- Better to have false starts than no starts at all.
- Take risks, don't expect perfection!
- Stop doing the good things and start focusing on the "great things."
- Focus on what is important in developing a community of learners. Use student learning data to drive all professional development.
- Systematic change with supports in changing culture.
- Embedded, effective ongoing professional development (in our schools, in our classrooms, in the hallways, in the like-minded schools, at the district level).
- Administrators (principal) as the instructional/transformational leader.
- Our district follows the model of guidance to independence, which promotes leaders amongst leaders, teachers as leaders.
- Cognitive coaching is evident from the district level, to the school level, to the classroom level including inter-school coaching.
- Research-based practices are evident in every school where all staff have established an instructional focus from the external and internal data collected (reading comprehension, writing, literacy, and higher-level thinking skills to name a few).
- High levels of accountability are a priority from the district to each of the schools.
- Data are collected, graphed, discussed, and monitored on a regular basis.
- The simple questions, "How are we improving student achievement, and what is the evidence we can see?" are asked of all who work in the district. (All departments focus on this question to improve their service—transportation,

---

(Continued)

(Continued)

> accounting, budget, maintenance, schools, each classroom teacher, etc.).
>
> • As a district of 208 schools, we are speaking the same language in reference to our instructional focus, and have commonality in utilizing the research to positively impact the work in the classroom to expect "Superb Results for All Students!"
>
> • For sustained systemic change, we all must be pointing in the same direction.
>
> • The district is committed to the work, and support is offered to every school.

Leaders Pose Complex, Essential Questions

At Glenora School, one of the elementary schools in Edmonton, Alberta, Canada, Principal Mary Michailides builds on, extends, and works to implement what the superintendent has created.

Following are some "essential questions" she asks of herself:

1. How can my supervision of staff enhance instruction in my school?

2. What feedback will I gather in my one-on-ones with my staff?

3. How will I encourage collaboration among my staff?

4. What are the components of instructional leadership?

5. How often will I spend time in my classrooms and with students to support the work of my staff?

6. How will I provide staff with feedback from my intervisitations in their classrooms?

7. In what ways will I work with my staff to ensure student potential is maximized?

8. How will I keep myself motivated as a "supervisor"?

9. What evidence will I accept in wanting to make a difference?

10. How am I modeling the expectations I have of my staff?

11. What do I value in my position and how do I live that?

12. How do I celebrate the successes with my staff? What are we doing to encourage each other in times of challenge?

She also believes that it is necessary for classroom teachers to take the time to answer self-reflective questions that move student learning forward. Such essential questions include the following:

13. What curricular outcomes would we like to see our students master and how are we sharing this information with our students?

14. How do we encourage and support self-directed learning: learning that becomes meaningful for each of our students?

15. What does good learning look like in our classroom/instructional environments?

16. How are we increasing students' level of responsibility and how are we providing them feedback?

17. What data are we gathering from student work?

18. What are my skills in gathering a balanced assessment profile, and what resources can assist me?

19. What are my plans for the collection of data that will be used to assess and evaluate student achievement? How am I involving my students in this process?

20. What evaluation criteria are being used? How are students made aware of the criteria and how are we involving our students in developing those criteria?

21. How are we focusing on student self-directed evaluation?

22. How do we manage a variety of instructional strategies that will motivate student learning and simulate real life?

23. What are we doing to encourage and develop an appetite for knowledge?

24. What do we do to inspire creativity, and create masters of problem solving in a complex world?

25. What daily evidence do you glean from your successful teaching experiences?

And finally:

26. How do I know I have made a difference?

Ways Leaders Can Deter and Diminish Self-Directed Learning

Following are some well-intended but "other-directed" mistakes school administrators will want to avoid:

- Creating a sense of dependency with staff by providing them with all the answers they would ever need to solve any problem.
- Having no or an unclear vision of the direction in which we are heading.
- Feeling that as an administrator, I need to control everything rather than relinquishing control but not responsibility.
- Resisting the acceptance and invitation of challenging situations.
- Discouraging taking risks.
- Forgetting to model risk-taking for your own staff.
- Not learning from making mistakes.
- Micromanaging.
- Creating an atmosphere in which the fear of evaluation limits the possibilities for innovation.
- Using punishments and rewards for actions with which you disagree or agree.
- Limiting choices.

Evaluation of performance, merit rating, or annual review.

It nourishes short-term performance, annihilates long-term planning, builds fear, demolishes teamwork, nourishes rivalry and politics.

It leaves people bitter, crushed, bruised, desolate, despondent, dejected, feeling inferior, some even depressed, unfit for work for weeks after receipt of rating, unable to comprehend why they are inferior. It is unfair, as it ascribes to the people in a group differences that may be caused totally by the system that they work in.

—W. Edwards Deming, *Out of Crisis*

Principles of Constructivism Guide the Self-Directed Community

Meaning-making is not a spectator sport. Knowledge is a constructive process. The activity of constructing content is what gets stored in memory. Humans don't *get* ideas; they *make* ideas.

Constructivism is a theory of learning based on a belief that human beings have an innate need to make meaning of their experiences. When humans are perplexed by anomalies, discrepancies, or new information, they have a natural inclination to make sense of it. This process of making sense is enhanced in environments when certain teaching behaviors are practiced, such as seeking and valuing students' points of view, challenging their suppositions, focusing on "big" ideas and long-range outcomes, creating conditions for self-assessment, and providing opportunities for reflection on experience.

The following twelve principles of constructivism guide teachers. The development of these descriptors has been informed by the work of several researchers and theoreticians, including Sigel (1984), Kuhn (1962), Dewey (1938), and Brooks and Brooks (2001).

1. Constructivist environments encourage self-directedness.

Autonomy empowers the pursuit of making connections among ideas and concepts. When students raise issues and frame questions, then analyze and answer those issues and questions themselves, they take responsibility for their own learning, becoming problem solvers and problem finders. In the pursuit of new understandings, they are led by their own ideas and informed by the ideas of others.

As such, constructivist environments must be safe as they provide freedom to experiment with ideas, explore issues, and encounter new information. When learners anticipate that their thoughts will be judged, their thinking mode shifts from open to closed. Nonjudgmental feedback encourages others to pursue their ideas more deeply and less defensively. Nonjudgmental feedback also helps students develop the capacity for evaluating the worth of their own and others' ideas. Listening to, paraphrasing, and clarifying ideas indicates that the other person's brain has the power to produce meaning.

2. Teachers view themselves as mediators of students' meaning-making.

Because learning is viewed as a continual process of engaging the mind that transforms the mind, constructivist teachers cast others in the role of producers of knowledge rather than consumers of knowledge. They see themselves as facilitators of meaning-making, interposing themselves between the learner and the learning so as to cause others to approach activities in a strategic way, to help them monitor their own progress in the learning, to construct meaning from the learning and from the process of learning, and then to apply the learnings to other contexts and settings.

Teachers' mediational questioning and problem posing stimulate the brain to engage in higher order and creative cognitive functions. Teachers help students raise and illuminate perplexing situations, problems to solve, discrepancies, and intriguing phenomena—the answers to which are not readily apparent. Day-to-day, real-life problems are the best way to practice problem solving.

Constructivist teachers seek elaboration of initial responses. Initial responses are just that: *initial.* People's first thoughts about issues are not necessarily their final thoughts or their best thoughts. Inviting elaboration causes students to reconceptualize and assess their own language, concepts, and strategies.

In dialogue, constructivist teachers use cognitive terminology. The words we hear and use in dialogue affect our way of thinking and ultimately our actions. Teachers deliberately choose words intended to activate and engage mental processes. Finding relationships, predicting outcomes, analyzing, and synthesizing are mental processes that require others to draw forth their knowledge, make connections, and create new understandings.

3. Constructivist approaches begin with raw data and direct experiences from which abstractions can be made.

Concepts, theorems, laws, criteria, and guidelines are abstractions that the human mind generates through interaction with previous information, new ideas, experiences, and data. The constructivist approach draws on primary sources, information from memory and past experiences, manipulatives, and real-life situations. Then, the constructivist approach helps learners generate abstractions from all of these data sources. Learners gather data from a variety of sources and are then asked to compare, analyze, synthesize, and evaluate. Learning becomes the result of research related to real problems.

Providing information is also valid for teachers. Providing information is appropriate when the information is linked (scaffolded) to previous learnings. Providing information is also appropriate when the learner expresses a need for the information and the data are then delivered in a manner that matches the learner's learning style. Data also should be relevant to the learner's developmental levels and drawn from multiple sources: visual, auditory, kinesthetic, and tactile. With a teacher's guidance, this data can then be acted upon and processed as the colleague makes inferences, forms concepts, synthesizes theorems, induces algorithms, generates laws, and creates guidelines so that learning is applied in and beyond the context in which it was learned.

4. Constructivism suggests a sequence of learning.

Constructivists such as Taba (1962), Bruner (1968), and Piaget (1969) believe that there is a sequence to concept formation in which learning begins with gathering sensory data, then making sense of the data by finding patterns and relationships, and then applying those concepts to new problems.

The first stage is the input, or "discovery," stage in which data are taken in through the senses and drawn from the memory of prior experiences. This is an open-ended opportunity to experiment and become familiar with materials and to generate questions and hypotheses.

Next is the processing stage, in which patterns are found, meaningful relationships are formed, and concepts are constructed from those data. New labels for concepts are formed, hypotheses are formed, and inferences are made.

Third is the output, or "concept application," stage. Further iterations of the discovery are made, then generalizations and principles are formed and used as models to explain problems and predict consequences in settings beyond the one in which the learning was formed.

5. Constructivist teachers challenge others' mental models.

Humans often develop and refine ideas about phenomena and then tenaciously hold on to these ideas as eternal truths. Much of what we think happens is determined by virtue of our agreement that it should, not because of close examination of our bounded assumptions, limited history, and existing mental models. Constructivist teachers realize that cognitive growth occurs when individuals revisit and reformulate a current perspective. Therefore, teachers provide data, present realities, and pose questions for the purpose of engendering contradictions to students' initial hypotheses, challenging present conceptions, illuminating another perspective, and breaching crystallized thinking. Teachers must listen to and understand the students' present conceptions or points of view to help them understand which notions might be accepted or rejected as contradictory.

6. Constructivist teachers support on-demand learning.

In the meaning-making process, humans direct the need for information in the moment. Because they feel a need for information or skills to fill the gaps and inadequacies in their process of meaning-making, there is a greater openness to learning. (Computers assist in this process as they allow the pursuit of interests through browsing, tapping varied databases in a random and nonlinear way. Teachers, therefore, allow students' responses to drive the interaction, shift the focus, and alter the content.)

Being alert to such verbal and nonverbal signals as eye movements; facial expressions; postural shifts; gestures; breathing rates; and changes in pitch, speed, and volume of speech, as well as overt expressions of interest and enthusiasm, the teacher may shift the topic or approach. (We all know of a "teachable moment" when our planned lesson was derailed by an event of greater interest.) Learners' in-the-moment insights, experiences, motivations, and interests may intersect around an urgent theme. When magnetic events exert an irresistible pull on a learner's mind, the teacher may hold his or her planned strategy in abeyance and "go with the flow."

7. Constructivism involves communities of learners.

Constructivist learning is a reciprocal process of the individual's influence on the group and the group's influence on the individual. Meaning-making is not only an individual operation. The individual also constructs meaning interactively with others' shared knowledge. Meaning-making may be an individual experience, one's unique way of constructing knowledge. Meaning-making also is a sociocultural phenomenon. Social processes of interaction and participation enhance, refine, and amplify meanings. An empowering way to change conceptions is to present one's own ideas to others as well as to hear and reflect on the ideas of others. Discourse among peers activates the meaning-making process. The constructivist environment encourages questioning of each other and rich dialogue within and among groups and teams of learners as they resolve differences in perceptions and styles and synthesize alternative viewpoints (Vygotsky, 1978).

8. Process is the content with constructivism.

A constructivist curriculum challenges the basic educational views of "knowledge" and "learning" with which most schools are comfortable. It causes us to expand our focus from educational outcomes, which are primarily collections of subskills. A constructivist curriculum embraces successful processes of participation in socially organized activities and the development of students' identities as conscious, flexible, efficacious, interdependent, and continual learners.

A constructivist curriculum lets go of having learners acquire predetermined meaning and has faith in the processes of individuals' construction of shared meanings through social interaction. Constructivist teachers, therefore, inquire about their students' understandings of concepts before sharing their own understandings of those concepts. When teachers share their ideas and theories before students have an opportunity to develop their own, questioning of theories is essentially eliminated. Students assume that the teacher knows more than they do. Consequently, they most often stop thinking about a concept or theory once they hear "the correct answer."

9. Constructing meaning takes time.

As such, constructivist teachers invite students to construct relationships and create metaphors. When sufficient time is given to activities, learners go beyond initial relationships to create novel relationships, find patterns, and generate theories for themselves. This also means that teachers allow wait time after posing questions.

With constructivism, failures are never dismissed as mistakes. Rather, time is taken to reflect on their learning, to compare intended with actual outcomes, to analyze and draw causal relationships, to synthesize meanings, and to apply their learnings to novel situations.

Unlike many other quick-fix educational innovations and experiments, constructivism remains focused on the longer view. Constructivist educators realize that assisting others to habituate self-directed learning takes years of well-defined instruction with qualified teachers and carefully constructed curriculum before a significant and enduring change is observed.

We know that the amount of time on task affects learning. As self-directed learning becomes a goal of education, greater value is placed on allocating time for learning activities intended to stimulate and practice the construction of personal meaning.

10. Constructivist teachers invite metacognition.

They invite students to think about their thinking. Time is taken to plan for, monitor, and reflect on the thinking skills, problem-solving and decision-making processes, and the intellectual habits/dispositions that are accruing. They invite colleagues to share their metacognition—to reveal their intentions, strategies, and plans for solving a problem; to describe their mental maps for monitoring their strategy during the problem solving; and to reflect on the strategy to determine its adequacy.

11. Assessment is viewed as another opportunity to accelerate self-directed learning.

In the constructivist environment, what matters most is whether the inhabitants are learning to become increasingly more self-managing, self-monitoring, and self-modifying. Teachers help students design diverse ways of gathering, organizing, and reporting evidence of continual learning and meaning-making.

The intent of constructivist assessment is to provide rich feedback to students that helps them to continue their learning journey. The emphasis is on making certain that judging the quality of work is a significant part of learning. Therefore, judging work, guided by well-designed rubrics that set forth quality criteria, is a collaborative experience between teacher and student and between student and student. Teachers require students to evaluate their own work before turning it in. Teachers expect that the student would be able to score the work in the same way that they do. When there is a discrepancy between the student's score and the teacher's score, a conference is needed. The conference establishes the worldview of both teacher and student. On that basis, discrepancies are resolved, standards are reinforced, and improvement goals are set.

Self-knowledge is the first step in self-assessment. Much of the work of self-evaluation is developed through the metacognitive process of reflection. This process of self-assessment provides internal and external data that promote one's own learning and growth.

12. Modeling is the most basic form of constructivist learning.

Teachers, parents, and administrators realize the importance of their own display of desirable learning behaviors in the presence of others with whom they work. If teachers want their students to value inquiry, then they must also value it. If teachers pose questions with the orientation that there is only one correct response, then how can students be expected to develop either the interest in or the analytic skills necessary for more diverse modes of inquiry?

In day-to-day events, and when problems arise in schools, class-rooms, and homes, the same types of constructivist learnings described above can be used. Without this consistency, there is likely to be a credibility gap. As Mahatma Gandhi said, "You must be the change you wish to see in the world."

These principles of constructivism may serve as a basis for under-standing why teachers who embrace the principles of self-directed learning do what they do. They provide the theoretical underpinnings of a model of human meaning-making. These principles also may be used as a template to determine the degree to which schools embrace a constructivist philosophy and as a vision that thought-full schools might strive to achieve.

Building a Self-Directed Community for Learning: A Self-Assessment Checklist

Applying the principles of constructivism requires constant oversight. It requires significant changes in the habits of all members of the community—board of education, school personnel, students, parents. To make these changes operable and real, we have developed a set of assumptions about people who are self-directed, and then self-assessment checklists that can be filled out by individuals as well as groups within the community.

Our assumptions are that self-directed people:

- Constantly search for alignment and congruence between their values and their actions
- Act with intentionality

	DOMAINS		
ATTRIBUTES OF SELF-DIRECTED PEOPLE	**Intentionally Self-Mediating**	**Mediating Self-Directedness in Others**	**Cultivating Self-Directedness in the Learning Organization**
Self-Managing			
Self-Monitoring			
Self-Modifying			

Figure 4.1   Domains and Attributes of Self-Directed People

- Contribute to and learn from others
- Seek alternative perspectives beyond their own
- Strive for continuous learning, growth, and improvement
- Reflect on and learn from experience
- Generate reciprocity among self, groups, and larger systems

We believe that self-directed people are

- Self-managing,
- Self-monitoring, and
- Self-modifying.

This assessment tool, therefore, is in the form of a checklist incorporating these three attributes in three domains:

- Intentionally self-mediating
- Mediating self-directedness in others
- Cultivating self-directedness in the learning organization

Self-Assessing/Self-Modifying Our Craft of Teaching

Professional educators continually experiment, inquire, test, gather data, revise, and modify their thoughts and practices. Continual learning constitutes career-long agendas for professional growth. Coaching, teaching standards, peer review, collaboration with other professionals, and seeking consultation from experts helps teachers integrate, extend, and apply this information in their classroom work.

Intentionally Self-Mediating

Self-Managing	Often	Sometimes	Not Yet
• Draws from prior knowledge, sensory data, and intuition to guide, hone, and refine actions			
• Displays an internal locus of control			
• Thoughtfully plans and initiates actions			
• Manages time effectively			
• Produces new knowledge through own research and experimentation			
• Uses clear and precise language			
• Balances solitude and togetherness, action and reflection, and personal and professional growth			
• Displays a sense of humor			

Self-Monitoring	Often	Sometimes	Not Yet
• Seeks perspectives beyond self and others to develop thoughtful responses			
• Generates new and innovative ideas and problem-solving strategies			
• Pursues ambiguities and possibilities to create new meanings			
• Manages self in relation to group			
• Is aware of what is known and not known and develops strategies to fill in the gaps			
• Evaluates, corrects, and adjusts work to improve its quality			

Figure 4.2 *(Continued)*

(Continued)

Self-Modifying	Often	Sometimes	Not Yet
• Explores choice points between self-assertion and integration with others			
• Seeks feedback from appropriate sources for improved performance			
• Reflects on and learns from experiences			
• Continues to learn new skills and strategies			
• Thoughtfully receives feedback and acts upon it			

Figure 4.2   Intentionally Self-Mediating People

Teaching frameworks such as Charlotte Danielson's (1996) *Framework for Teaching* and the California State Department of Education's (1997) Standards for the Teaching Profession are useful resources for helping teachers reflect on their own practices. Such standards, in the form of rubrics, provide a scale for teachers to reflect on and assess their own performance and make commitments for greater personal mastery. After they describe how a standard might sound or look in their classrooms, teachers set goals related to where their teaching fits in the continuum of development. Self-directed teachers ask themselves, "What might I do to achieve a next higher level of competency?" Master teachers are never complacent about their performance; they always have more to learn (Sawyer, 2003).

Self-directed teachers generate their own data through action research. The most convincing data are not reports of distant and historical research but teachers' own results from using new processes and approaches in their classrooms with their own students and subject matter. Teachers can establish and employ techniques of data collection to assess the results on student behavior and performance when they use new processes or standards.

Serving as critical friends in a safe and trusting environment, teachers may observe one another as they apply teaching standards in their classrooms. Figure 4.5 shows a form suggested by Robert and Sue Garmston (2002)[1] that may assist teams of teachers in their observation of each other.

Mediating Self-Directedness in Others

Self-Managing	Often	Sometimes	Not Yet
• Maintains faith in own abilities to mediate and enhance other's capacities for self-directedness			
• Poses questions and effectively employs language tools to cause others to think through problems for themselves			
• Effectively builds and maintains a trusting relationship with others			
• Values and incorporates instruction in cooperative strategies and group problem solving			

Self-Monitoring	Often	Sometimes	Not Yet
• Envisions self-directed behaviors in others and employs own language and strategies to achieve vision			
• Employs multiple strategies for self-evaluation depending on readiness, style, and learning preferences of others			
• Provides time and tone for reflection			

Self-Modifying	Often	Sometimes	Not Yet
• Continues to hone and refine skills of mediating self-directedness in others			
• Contributes to and continually learns from group members and from the group interaction			
• Experiments with and revises group strategies based upon feedback			
• Uses assessment results to make choices about the need to change			

Figure 4.3   Mediating Self-Directedness in Others

Self-Managing	Often	Sometimes	Not Yet
• Is motivated by and committed to achieving shared goals			
• Uses past successes to inform future practice			
• Productively manages the tensions between the vision of the desired state and the realities of the existing state			
• Assists the group to prioritize and focus its resources where they can make the greatest impact			
• Assists the group to access a wide repertoire of thinking and process skills			
• When problems arise, works to generate and use multiple options for moving ahead			
• Honors and uses diversity within the group			
• Assists group to invent, refine, and employ process tools			
• Volunteers services in behalf of the group			

Self-Monitoring	Often	Sometimes	Not Yet
• Develops group's awareness of what it doesn't know, needs to know, and develops strategies for attainment			
• Helps group surface and become aware of its assumptions and knowledge that may interfere with its learning			
• Assists group to become aware of what it knows and needs to know and helps to develop strategies for attainment			

Figure 4.4 *(Continued)*

(Continued)

Self-Monitoring	Often	Sometimes	Not Yet
• Facilitates group to become aware of and apply criteria for decision making			
• Creates feedback spirals and monitoring systems based on core values and organizing principles			
• Facilitates group process in reflecting on and assessing its processes and products			
• Regards knowledge and knowing as fluid, provisional, and subject to improvement from information outside itself			

Self-Modifying	Often	Sometimes	Not Yet
• Assists group to reframe its decisions and activities based on new data			
• Assists groups to create, apply, calibrate, and refine performance and product standards			
• Continuously refines inter- and intragroup communications			
• Regards disagreement and conflict as sources of learning and transformation for self and group			
• Honors the pathways from novice to expert in performance			
• Values group interactions and trusts the processes of dialogue			
• Networks with others to create webs of interconnectedness and mutual influence			
• Strives to develop and honor shared norms and group identity			
• Clarifies group's mission, goals, intentions, and outcomes			

Figure 4.4   Cultivating Self-Directedness in the Learning Organization

STANDARD: _____

WHAT WOULD YOU SEE THE TEACHER DOING? WHAT WOULD YOU HEAR THE TEACHER SAYING?	WHAT WOULD YOU SEE STUDENTS DOING? WHAT WOULD YOU HEAR THEM SAYING?	WHAT WOULD YOU SEE IN THE CLASSROOM?

Figure 4.5   Teaching Standards Peer Observation Form

After a conference in which the standards are selected and operationalized, the observing teachers can collect evidence of indicators of the performance of such standards. During a reflective conference, share the data, allow the teacher to self-assess, and plan for achieving the next higher level of performance along the continuum.

Self-Directed Teachers Manage, Monitor, and Modify Themselves

Self-directed learning is not just "kids' stuff." Teachers as professionals grow in their dispositions and behaviors of self-directedness along with their students.

Following are three assessment scales intended to cause self-reflection, self-evaluation, and self-modification (see Figure 4.6).

Assessing Your Own Dispositions of Self-Directed Learning

In Chapter 2, we described the dispositions of self-directed learners. Read the following questions and rate yourself on a scale of 1 to 10. Provide evidence to support your rating. Be honest, but don't be too hard on yourself. Through practice and self-monitoring, self-directedness can be learned. The more you practice, the more self-directed you will become.

The checklist in Figure 4.7 invites you to assess the degree to which you are focusing on and teaching the dispositions of self-directedness to your students and to what degree they are performing them. The intent is for you to self-assess your student's performance of the dispositions and then to make an even greater effort to discuss, label, reinforce, and activate these dispositions. The ultimate goal is to have students manage, monitor, and modify their own applications of the dispositions.

The following checklist is intended to help teachers assess and reflect on their own instruction to determine if they are including self-directed learning as a conscious goal of their curriculum and instruction. There may be some areas in which much emphasis is placed, while other areas may need more concerted effort to move from "not yet" to "sometimes," or from "sometimes" to "often."

Summary

Self-directed learning must take place in a community that encourages self-modifying, self-managing, and self-monitoring. Application of the principles of constructivism creates the foundation for such a community. We have developed a set of indicators that describe the behaviors of

Self-Managing

1. I manage my impulses and am willing to delay gratification in order to attain long-term goals. I make sure I know the parameters, requirements, directions, and criteria before I begin. I have a clear vision in mind of what I'm doing, where I'm going, how to get there, and how I will know when I've arrived.

   Not yet, but I'm learning   —1—2—3—4—5—6—7—8—9—10   *I usually behave this way.*

   Evidence:

2. I am a flexible thinker—I seek new ways of looking at things, can change my mind, and can take on different perspectives. I approach problems knowing there are alternative definitions of the problem and therefore alternative solutions. I can look at the bigger, long-range picture as well as the "micro-view" analyzing details and the parts that make up the whole.

   Not yet, but I'm learning   —1—2—3—4—5—6—7—8—9—10   *I usually behave this way.*

   Evidence:

3. I am curious and am not afraid to ask questions, I am conscious of the questions I ask, and know how to design them to search for data to support conclusions and to inquire into intriguing ideas. I am alert to problems and strive to define and refine them to a workable solution.

   Not yet, but I'm learning   —1—2—3—4—5—6—7—8—9—10   *I usually behave this way.*

   Evidence:

4. I have a rich storehouse of information and experiences and, when I am confronted with a problem, I draw on past knowledge and apply it to new situations. I reflect on, learn from, and apply my past knowledge, and can transfer skills and knowledge to new and novel situations. I learn from my mistakes and consider them opportunities for learning.

   Not yet, but I'm learning   —1—2—3—4—5—6—7—8—9—10   *I usually behave this way.*

   Evidence:

5. I use all my senses (visual, kinesthetic, auditory, tactile, gustatory, olfactory) in order to learn. I maximize the intake of information by using my senses of vision, movement, hearing, touch, taste, and smell.

Figure 4.6 (*Continued*)

(Continued)

Not yet, but I'm learning   —1—2—3—4—5—6—7—8—9—10   *I usually behave this way.*

Evidence:

6.   I am a creative person and know how to generate products and elaborate ideas. I know how to engage my mind so that I can produce original ideas and products by thinking fluently, flexibly.

Not yet, but I'm learning   —1—2—3—4—5—6—7—8—9—10   *I usually behave this way.*

Evidence:

Self-Monitoring

7.   I listen to myself and am aware of my own thoughts (metacognition) and feelings. I strive to be aware of my own assumptions and reactions to situations and to others. I try to be aware of my effects on others and on the environment.

Not yet, but I'm learning   —1—2—3—4—5—6—7—8—9—10   *I usually behave this way.*

Evidence:

8.   I am a persistent person. If I don't succeed on the first try, I keep trying until I do succeed. I know how to turn to resources to help me when I get stuck. I monitor my own problem-solving strategies and know how and when to generate others if one is not working for me.

Not yet, but I'm learning   —1—2—3—4—5—6—7—8—9—10   *I usually behave this way.*

Evidence:

9.   I check my work for quality and try to be accurate and precise in whatever I do. I value craftsmanship, fidelity, and exactness in my ideas, communications, and products.

Not yet, but I'm learning   —1—2—3—4—5—6—7—8—9—10   *I usually behave this way.*

Evidence:

10.   I listen to others with understanding and empathy. I can set aside my own solutions, value judgments, and personal thoughts in order to devote my mind to others. I can listen skillfully by paraphrasing, clarifying, and remaining silent while others are speaking.

Figure 4.6 (*Continued*)

(Continued)

>   *Not yet, but I'm learning*   *—1—2—3—4—5—6—7—8—9—10*   *I usually behave this way.*

Evidence:

Self-Modifying

11.   I think about my words and choose them so as to communicate my ideas precisely. If I detect that I am not being understood, I modify my words, metaphors, and examples to clarify what I mean. I strive to constantly build and expand my vocabulary.

>   *Not yet, but I'm learning*   *—1—2—3—4—5—6—7—8—9—10*   *I usually behave this way.*

Evidence:

12.   I find the world to be an awesome place. I get a sense of euphoria from my craft. I am curious and have a sense of wonderment about the world in which I live. I enjoy solving problems and always try to do my best.

>   *Not yet, but I'm learning*   *—1—2—3—4—5—6—7—8—9—10*   *I usually behave this way.*

Evidence:

13.   I am a continual learner. I reflect on and learn from my experiences and easily admit that I don't know but am eager to find out. I am never complacent about my current level of performance but always strive to learn more.

>   *Not yet, but I'm learning*   *—1—2—3—4—5—6—7—8—9—10*   *I usually behave this way.*

Evidence:

Figure 4.6   An Inventory to Assess Your Own Dispositions of Self-Directedness

self-directed people in a variety of contexts. As school systems use these indicators to guide their work, they will begin to develop a new set of behaviors. A significant change in the behavior of people in a learning community will deeply affect the beliefs and attitudes of that community. As a result, a more empowered and self-directed community of learners will face the constant dilemmas and challenges of our 21st century.

In my classroom: **DISPOSITIONS OF SELF-DIRECTED LEARNERS**	**We have not touched on this disposition**	**We refer to this disposition on occasion**	**We regularly practice this disposition**	**Students monitor their own use of this disposition**
Self-Managing				
1. The management of impulsivity				
2. Thinking flexibly				
3. Questioning				
4. Applying past knowledge				
5. Gathering data				
6. Imagining, creating, innovating				
Self-Monitoring				
7. Awareness of our own thinking (metacognition)				
8. Persisting				
9. Monitoring accuracy and precision				
10. Listening to others with understanding and empathy				
Self-Modifying				
11. Thinking and communicating with clarity and precision				
12. Responding with wonderment and awe				
13. Continuous learning				

Figure 4.7   Teaching the Intellectual Dispositions of Self-Directed Learning

OBSERVABLE INDICATORS	OFTEN	SOMETIMES	NOT YET
I teach toward self-directed learning.			
I consciously develop lessons intended to engage students' thinking processes and self-directed learning.			
I hear myself employing the terminology of self-directed learning in my discussions with students.			
I communicate with parents about their child's growth in thinking and self-directed learning.			
I recognize and reinforce students when they display the dispositions of self-directedness.			
If you were to come into my classroom, you would see indicators of my students' self-directed learning.			
If you were to come into my classroom, you would see indicators of my teaching toward self-directedness.			
I am aware of and assess students' increasing growth in self-directed learning.			
I value and teach students how to assess their own growth toward self-directed learning.			

Figure 4.8   How Am I Doing?

Note

1. For an expanded discussion of the role of leadership, see Lambert (2003) and Lambert et al. (2002).

CHAPTER 5

The Teacher's Role in Self-Directed Learning

Students often come from previous schools and classrooms and home environments in which evaluation, rewards, and accountability are external. Students will need to understand the significance of self-evaluation and the role it can play in their learning process. In this chapter, we will show how teachers mediate students' self-directedness through designing instruction lessons, units, and activities; by creating classroom conditions for self-directed learning; by engaging and enhancing reflective dialogue; and by serving as a model for students to emulate.

> Teachers open the door, but you must enter by yourself.
>
> —Chinese Proverb

Mediating for Self-Directed Learning

Mediate comes from the word *middle.* A mediator interposes him- or herself in the middle between a person and some event, problem, conflict, or other perplexing situation that needs resolution. According to Reuven Feuerstein's (2000) "Mediated Learning Experience," the mediator may intervene in such a way as to enhance the three phases of self-directed learning:

Self-Managing: to assist the person in approaching a problem with clarity of outcomes, and a strategic plan that includes past experiences, anticipates indicators of success, and includes a thoughtful exploration of creative alternatives.

Self-Monitoring: to assist the person in establishing metacognitive strategies that will alert the perceptions for in-the-moment clues and indicators as to whether the strategic plan is working or not, and to assist in the decision-making process connected with altering the plan.

Self-Modifying: to assist the person in reflecting on, evaluating, analyzing, and constructing meaning from the experience and to apply the learning to future situations.

The ultimate goal of the mediator is to modify the person's intellectual capabilities for self-directed learning—to help the person become self-managing, self-monitoring, and self-modifying, with no need for intervention from others.

Designing Student Work for Self-Directed Learning

Teachers constantly make decisions about what tasks, projects, and problems they assign to students that will engage and promote their learning. Teachers consider such things as the amount of time it will take to complete the project, the resources that are available in the school and community, the standards to which the projects might relate, the conceptual learning that

> Education is not preparation for life; education is life itself.
>
> —John Dewey

can accrue, the developmental levels of the students, and their capacities for working together and independently. We would also suggest that a critical consideration is whether instruction is designed to provide opportunities for students to be self-directed.

This level of intentional design for self-directed learning has some key attributes, such as the following:

Planning: Students should be included in planning for a given project or assignment. They should be involved in clarifying the goals, thinking about time management, and establishing criteria in accordance with standards. If students and teachers agree upon shared indicators of how well the process works as well as what a quality product will look like, the chances of achieving that product are greatly improved. The work should produce some relevant, authentic, and tangible products that have significance and meaning for the student. The design of the product and the production process should be left to student choice as long as the product will meet the established criteria.

Audience: Students need to be exposed to feedback from resources outside of the classroom. When this is possible, the teacher can play the role of coaching for a high-quality performance and the audience can serve as the evaluators. Such audiences might include the following:

Teachers other than the one who is teaching the class

Parents and/or members of the community

Experts in the subject being studied

Peers

Feedback: Learning requires continual direct feedback given throughout the production process as close to the performance and as timely as possible so the student can be in a continuous spiral of learning. During the process of developing the product, the standards, criteria, and rubrics should be monitored and revisited with invitations for students to make comparisons and judgments about the degree to which the standards are being met. Students can be given feedback from peers, critical friends, the teacher, or other expert resources. The quality of the feedback should be neutral and without value judgments. If students are to become self-evaluative, then the teacher and peers must remain nonevaluative so as not to rob learners of opportunities to evaluate themselves and their own efforts against a set of criteria.

If the criteria for progress and product are not adequately being met, the student is offered additional opportunities to complete the product without sanctions. The consequence of successful or unsuccessful effort should be the same—a careful review of what went well and what did not. When students know that, they have a greater chance of learning from the experience.

Collaboration: Tasks should be designed to encourage cooperation, teaming, and sharing of responsibilities. Through this interaction, the group and the individual continue to grow. Listening, consensus seeking, giving up an idea to work with someone else's, empathy, compassion, group leadership, knowing how to support group efforts, altruism—all are behaviors indicative of cooperative human beings. How well a group works together directly influences the quality of the product. This relationship and the behaviors that produced the group's productivity should be explored and constantly monitored.

Diversity: Products should invite variety, creativity, novel approaches, and differences in styles and approaches. The range and variety of approaches leads to greater empathy, flexibility, creativity, and expanded insights.

Authentic Processes: The methods of inquiry and the conditions under which the work is done should parallel and replicate the methods inherent in the discipline (For example, in studying an historical event, students would experience the methods of the historian. In science, students would engage in scientific inquiry. In art, students would work as artists.)

Choice: Students should be allowed to choose topics, methods, time, sequence of steps, access to resources, and so on. Sometimes choice is limited because of time or resources. Such circumstances provide opportunities for creative efforts and divergent thinking to accomplish the task under adverse conditions.

Developmentally appropriate: The content and processes of production should be appropriate to students' maturity levels, experiences, background, and cultural diversity.

Interdisciplinary[1]: The work should engage the students in a variety of disciplines—mathematical, historical, scientific, creative, and more. The project should provide opportunities to

Count and measure. This is the authentic origin of mathematics. It leads students to explore their experience in terms of what numbers can reveal about reality.

Control variables. This launches scientific investigation. What happens if they change certain variables? How will that affect the results? Can they predict what will happen?

Determine who else has ever had this experience. This invites students to experience methods of inquiry across the disciplines and the search for primary and secondary sources of information.

Investigate what others have written or reported about it. This opens the door to reading, which puts us in touch with the thoughts of those who have gone before us, charting the way and establishing the content.

Communicate with others about the experience. Serious learners have a responsibility to share what they learn with others. Making themselves clearly understood is the basis of effective communication: oral, written, visual, and dramatic.

Compare this experience with other experiences they have had. This prompts students to look across the disciplines, to discover relationships and connections with other experiences in their lives. This is the process by which meaning is defined and understanding is cultivated.

Embellish, enhance, and leave their mark on this experience. This is the transformational opportunity for creativity in which each person generates and contributes to his or her own experiences and those of others.

Reflection: Upon completion of the activity, time should be provided to reflect on, evaluate, and learn from the process of production, collaboration, and inquiry. This might be done in written journals and/or oral dialogues. The amount of time for reflection should be at least equal to the amount of time invested in planning. Students might reflect on which of the dispositions of self-direction they drew upon and what this experience has taught them about themselves, their responsibilities, and their place in the world. What personal learning can they carry forth to future situations? Everything learned in any subject should reveal something about who they are and their place in the world.

Transference and applicability: As part of the reflection process, commitments should be explored as to how the learning from this process may be applied in other settings in school, life, work, home, other classes, and/or the community. Students should be invited to reflect on which behaviors might be modified, strengthened, or even extinguished to better produce achievement in the future. This bridging or transference is essential for learning to be "cemented" and internalized.

Martin Heiddeger suggests that learning is an engagement of the mind that changes the mind. These design qualities provide challenge, engagement, and motivation: the kind of work in which students are willing and eager to engage and from which they will naturally learn.

Figure 5.1 is an assessment instrument intended to assure that the student understands and the teacher agrees that the student understands the self-directed learning criteria for the project or task.

Creating Classroom Conditions That Enhance Openness to Continuous Learning

Evaluation is a conversation between the internal and the external criteria. If the external criteria do not match the learner's criteria, evaluative judgments will not be likely to change performance. Although students may work for the grade, they may not internalize learning for the future. For example, many students respectfully go through the writing process in their English classes, yet when they

Student and Teacher Project Criteria Assessment Checklist[i]			
Name of Task _____	Student Name _____		
Criteria appropriate for the task ✓	Thinking about my work	Student assessment ✓	Teacher assessment ✓
	SELF-MANAGING		
	1. I have a good idea of what I am supposed to do, and I can explain it in my own words.		
	2. I can think of and list different ways to do this task.		
	3. I have considered how my strengths and learning preferences will help me complete this task.		
	SELF-MONITORING		
	4. I can describe my plan for completing the task.		
	5. I have a way to track my progress along my plan.		
	6. I understand how my work will be assessed.		
	7. I am able to use the rubric as a guide to evaluate my own work and the work of others.		
	8. I have drawn upon or adapted methods and strategies that I have used before to help me complete this task.		
	SELF-MODIFYING		
	9. In completing my tasks I have considered the following questions: • What did I do? • What could I have done instead? • What will I do next time?		

Figure 5.1 *(Continued)*

(Continued)

Criteria appropriate for the task ✓	Thinking about my work	Student assessment ✓	Teacher assessment ✓
	10. My plan worked and I can explain why.		
	11. I have considered different ways in which to communicate my work.		
	12. I have considered my personal learning goals to improve my work on this task.		
	13. I have thought of other tasks and situations in which my learnings may be applied.		
	14.		
	15.		
	16.		

Figure 5.1   Project Criteria Checklist

SOURCE: Adapted with permission from Foster, Graham, Evelyn Sawicki, Hyacinth Schaeffer, and Victor Zelinski. (2002). *I think, therefore I learn*. Markham, Ontario, Canada: Pembroke Publishers Limited.

are required to write college applications, they do not use the writing process. When questioned, they often reply, "That was stuff we did in class—I never did see why we had to revise our drafts." We want the conversation between internal criteria—what I value as important in my work—and external criteria—what you value in my work— to provide the basis for a conversation about what constitutes good work. Learners must be open to feedback. They must be able to trust that the purpose of evaluation is not a game of "gotcha" but is an honest response that provides information to consider in the revision process. Learners need the humility of realizing that all work can be improved. In a classroom that is focused on self-directed learning, the purpose of evaluation is to provide critical feedback for improving performance. Critical feedback means that students will

- Respect the evaluator: Teachers must provide credible information to students about the quality of their work.

- Respect the criteria: Students must regard the criteria for judgment to be valid and consistent. They should know the criteria in advance so that their work can be targeted toward the criteria.

> A goal of education, therefore, is to assist growth toward greater complexity and integration and to assist in the process of self-organization—to modify individuals' capacity to modify themselves.
>
> —Reuven Feuerstein

However, feedback is only one half of the story for self-directed learners. The other half is how students receive the feedback and what they do with what they learn from it. Teachers need to work through levels of feedback as they build trust with their students. The levels of feedback might be seen through the framework provided by Johari's windows (Luft, 1984):

- Level one: *The open window: We both see what the problems with the work are.* The teacher and the student evaluate the work produced. They both are looking at the work with the same criteria. They agree on the evaluation of the work.
- Level two: *The blind window: The teacher sees what the problems are with the work, and the student does not see those problems.* In this instance, the teacher is bringing issues with the work to the student and the student may not see those same issues. At this point, the student is entering a place where she must receive feedback about something she is not aware of. The teacher must help the student receive and make sense out of that feedback, if she wants to see the student improve.
- Level three: *The hidden window: The student may know something about the work that the teacher has not seen.* Sometimes students have insights into their work that the teacher is not aware of. For example, the student may be taking a risk with this writing, possibly experimenting with dialogue, and the teacher may not recognize that intention. Harsh judgment of an experiment can cause the student to become more conservative in the next piece of work.
- Level four: *The unknown window: Neither the student nor the teacher sees something in the work until they examine it together in a conference.* There are times when the work reveals itself through closer examination and discussion. Just as literary text is often not understood completely by the author until there is an audience response, so it is with the text of student work. These new insights are greatly cherished by students because they are indicators of the respect and value the teacher places on their work.

We look at these as levels of engagement with students as the teacher moves students through feedback that provides increasingly more self-knowledge about their work. The levels get deeper as the trust builds in the students. As the trust builds for the students, their capacity for receiving and acting upon feedback is strengthened. Ultimately, this leads to a self-directed learner who knows how to use judgments and feedback from others to improve the work.

Dispositions for Giving and Receiving Feedback to Improve Work

When teachers build a learning community in which feedback is received, they must become good listeners. As Deborah Meier once stated, "Teaching is mostly listening. Learning is mostly telling." Following are some descriptions of teachers' dispositions that, when employed in the classroom, create a greater feeling of trust. These are the relational behaviors that protect students' vulnerability, encourage honesty and an openness to receiving feedback in an honest means of continuous learning.

Listening With Understanding and Empathy

Some examples of good listening might be prompted by the following:

- "Tell me about what you were thinking when you were developing this work."
- "What do you see as the strength in this work?"
- "I have made some comments about your work. Tell me how you understand those comments."
- "What do you need to consider as you work on improving your work?"

Examples of good listening when the class is engaged in the critique of work include the following:

- "As we listen to the author of this work, let's practice both warm and cool feedback. When we say 'warm' we mean feedback that recognizes the strength in the work. What we respond favorably toward. 'Cool' means feedback that is critical and, at the same time, helpful to improve the work."
- "How can we help Jose make this work even more powerful"
- "What strategies have you used that help you improve your work?"

Examples of good listening in peer critique:

- "How might the rubric help you to improve your work?"
- "Help me understand your thinking."
- "I understand what you are doing, and I especially liked this part of your work."

Thinking Flexibly

When you are considering a piece of work that needs to be improved, you must think flexibly. If what you are doing is not working, you need to open up to other possibilities. When experimenting in a science lab, you may need to try three or four different hypotheses. When faced with a math problem, you may need to try another strategy if the one you are using is not working. When in art class, you may need to sketch many different ideas before settling on the one you will finally take to the finish.

Allowing students to think flexibly, take the risk of playing with work, creates an atmosphere in which students learn that there is, after all, more than one way of doing things—and often more than one right answer.

Accepting One Another's Ideas Without Judgment

Although evaluation is ultimately about judgment, the classroom environment needs to be infused with coaching, instruction, and lots of constructive feedback in order for the evaluation to have real meaning. Effective assessment is instructional. It helps the student as well as the teacher understand where to go next in the work. There is a difference between formative assessments that provide lots of opportunities for learning and summative assessments that require the student to bring that learning together at a new level of synthesis.

Classrooms that offer considerable give and take about what makes good work and how to get there provide that instructional atmosphere. Students begin to realize that all of us, no matter where we are, continue to be works in progress. Keeping the fire lit for learning means not dampening it with negative judgment.

Getting Students Into the Habit of Self-Reflection

Maximizing meaning-making and self-evaluation is developed through the metacognitive process of reflection. To be reflective means to wander mentally through where you have been and to try to make some sense of it. The act of reflection, both alone and with a group, provides an opportunity for the following:

- Amplifying the meaning of one's work through the insights of others;
- Applying meaning beyond the situation in which it was learned;
- Making a commitment to modifications, plans, and experimentation; and
- Documenting learning and providing a rich base of shared knowledge.

The ultimate purpose of reflection is to get learners into the habit of thinking about their experiences. Once learners have developed this habit, they start hearing both an internal and an external voice of reflection. A goal of self-directed learning should be to habituate reflection, individually and collectively.

When asking students to reflect on their work, we must be aware that most of them have never been asked to do this before. They will need coaching and modeling to see how this works. Teaching reflection can start with simple activities and increase in complexity throughout the year.

The External Voice of Reflection

Sharing reflections on events validates, expands, and enriches our internal conversations. By sharing we can demonstrate and practice effective listening skills, probe for clarity and understanding, ask thoughtful questions, and share our metacognition. Some ways to develop the capacity for sharing reflections include sitting with fellow students in a circle and having each student offer one reflection on the day's activities, or sharing thoughts in small groups with a designated recorder who synthesizes the group's comments to present to the large group. Participants could then offer and analyze problem-solving strategies or share an example of a disposition or a habit of mind displayed by each group member.

Teachers, as mediators of students' self-directed learning, will, of course, pose powerful questions designed to cause the students to verbalize their reflections and to make meaning from their experiences. Such reflection may take place before, during, and after a learning activity. Schön (1983) refers to this as reflection *for* practice, reflection *in* practice, and reflection *on* practice.

Reflection on Self-Managing

Teachers can cause students to engage in reflection on self-managing. For example, if the intention is to have students draw forth cognitive, emotional information from visual, auditory, kinesthetic, and tactile input, the teacher may pose such questions as,

"How do you feel about this project?"

"How do you envision the final product?"

"In what activities will you engage to achieve your goals?"

"What questions are you asking yourself as you begin?"

If the intent is to link information to previous learnings, the teacher may pose such questions as,

"What do you already know about this topic as a base from which to start?"

"What, knowledge, insights, or prior learnings will you draw upon as you develop your project?"

Reflection on Self-Monitoring

Teachers can cause students to engage in reflection on self-monitoring. If the intent is to cause students to think about their thinking, about the completeness, satisfaction with, and interest in the reflective processes, the teacher may pose such questions as,

"What will you be aware of in your own decision-making process?"

"What were some of the criteria for excellence you were holding in your head to judge your own product?"

"How did this conversation with your teammates affect your thinking and planning on your project?"

Reflection on Self-Modifying

Teachers can cause students to engage in reflection on self-modifying. If the intent is to have students compare the results that were anticipated with the results that were achieved, the teacher may pose such questions as,

"How does this compare with how you thought it would turn out?"

"How does this compare with other data from other sources?"

If teachers want students to search for effects and find connections among possible causal factors, they may ask such questions as,

"How might you account for this?"

"What are some things that might be affecting this?"

If the teachers' intent is to cause the students to act on and process the information by analyzing, synthesizing, and evaluating, they may ask such questions as,

"What seems most important to consider?"

"What are some specific patterns or trends that seem to be emerging?"

"How is this similar to/different from _____?"

If the teacher's intent is to help students apply the learning to contexts beyond the one in which it was experienced and make commitments to plans of action, such questions as the following may be posed:

"What insights or learnings from this experience will you carry forth to similar situations?"

"In what other applications will you make use of these learnings?"

The real intent of these questions and the purpose of engaging in such conversations is to cause the learner to begin asking him- or herself these same types of questions. The goal is to shift the dialogue from being external to becoming internal—inside the mind of the learner.

Getting the External Dialogue Internal

Although these three components of self-directedness are presented in a "linear" fashion, this is not meant to imply a series of sequential steps. We enter and progress in a more random fashion, starting again, revisiting, retracing, and pausing to contemplate. What is in evidence, however, is a consciousness about where one is in the process.

> When the mind is thinking it is talking to itself.
>
> —Plato

When self-directed people confront some decision, problem, ambiguous situation, dilemma, or other paradoxical experience requiring skillful thinking, they often (a) develop a problem-solving strategy or plan of action, (b) maintain that plan in mind over a period of time, monitoring its progress to determine if it is producing the desired results, then (c) reflect back on and evaluate the plan upon its completion and incorporate the learning into a changed or expanded repertoire.

Planning a strategy before embarking on a course of action assists us in keeping track of the steps in the sequence of planned behavior at the conscious awareness level for the duration of the activity. It facilitates making temporal and comparative judgments; assessing the readiness for more or different activities; and monitoring our interpretations, perceptions, decisions, and behaviors. An example of this would be what superior teachers do daily: develop a teaching strategy for a lesson, keep that strategy in mind throughout the instruction, then reflect back upon the strategy to evaluate its effectiveness in producing the desired student outcomes. Self-directed people have an *internal locus of control*. They assume responsibility for their own successes or failures. A teacher might say, "As I consider the confusion I saw the students experiencing, I wondered whether my directions were sufficiently clear."

With repeated experiences, conversations about the problem-solving processes with others, mediation by a teacher or mentor, and personal reflection, the steps become internalized and habituated. When confronted with problematic situations, self-directed people begin an inner conversation by asking, "What is the most *intelligent thing* I can do right now?"

Internal Dialogue for Self-Managing

Self-managing people are deliberate; they have a plan of action before they begin. They have a goal in mind or an end product or vision available to them. They know what questions to ask to gather needed data, and they increasingly become aware of the temporal, environmental, financial, and human resources available to them. They might ask themselves such questions as,

"What are my goals and purposes—what am I trying to accomplish?"

"What information do I already have? What more do I need to know?"

"What might be some of the connections between this problem and other problems that I know exist or that could be contributing to this situation?"

"What are my resources, how can I draw on my past successes with problems like this?"

"How can I approach this problem *flexibly?* How might I look at the situation in another way, how can I draw upon my repertoire of problem-solving strategies, how can I look at this problem from a fresh perspective?"

"Who else might I turn to for help? How does this problem affect others; how can we solve it together, and what can I learn from others that would help me become a better problem solver?"

"How might I know when I have reached my goal?"

"How should I best sequence the steps of my strategies?"

"What's the best that can happen?"

Internal Dialogue for Self–Monitoring

Self-directed people try to be conscious of their actions, emotions, motives, beliefs, and values. Furthermore, they strive to increase their awareness of the effects their actions are having on other, on the task, and on the environment. As a result of what they observe, they modify their actions. They might ask themselves questions such as these:

"Which of my subgoals have been attained so far using my strategy?"

"What errors am I detecting and how can I recover from those errors, whether by making a quick fix or by retreating to the last known correct operation?"

"Which strategy should I choose that will reduce the possibility of error and will provide easy recovery?"

"What kinds of feedback will be available at various points, and how will I evaluate the usefulness of that feedback?"

"What has been done so far and what should come next?"

"What are some specific patterns or trends that I see emerging?"

Internal Dialogue for Self–Modifying

Even with this analysis, the self-directed conversation is not yet complete. The learnings must be constructed, synthesized, and applied or transferred to other learning contexts, content areas, or life situations. Some questions might be,

"What did I do well? How do I know I did it?"

"What can I do differently in the future to achieve better results?"

"What is most important for me to focus on in myself? How might I assess this?"

"If I could videotape this presentation, what would I want to see/hear in myself when it is replayed?"

"What might I learn from this task, and how might I know I've learned this?"

"How has this internal conversation supported my thinking?"

"How might I work to continue the thinking I've started?"

"In what other ways might I continue to support my learning?"

At this stage, the self-directed person takes new knowledge constructed through analysis and applies that knowledge to future situations. Experience can bring change, but experience alone is not enough. Experience is actually constructed: compared, differentiated, categorized, and labeled. This allows us to more efficiently recognize and more clearly interpret events, departures from routines, and novel occurrences. Thus, the self-directed person can predict the consequences of possible alternatives and activities with greater precision. Without this conceptual system people may view each experience as "episodic," they may approach tasks as if they have never experienced them before, they may feel inefficacious as problem solvers, and increasingly, their lives remain chaotic.

The test of truly internalizing these habits is to see what students do when you do not remind them of what to do. There should be times in the school year or in a course of study when students are given assignments without the prompts and reminders. For example, in a middle school, students were given a performance assessment designed to see how they approached research independently. The students were given a challenge to research any aspect of a given time period (e.g., the sixties) and report on their learning to the class. This assignment required that students

- Choose a topic of interest and narrow the research questions to a manageable few.
- Work cooperatively in a group, managing their time and their responsibilities to the group and identifying key areas for learning.
- Monitor the strategies they chose so that they could complete the task with high quality as well as in a timely manner.
- Develop their own criteria for what would constitute quality work.
- Make certain that they had outside readers for their work so that they could receive feedback.
- Revise their work.

The students were given an opportunity to do this work during class time. They were not allowed to take the work out of school. The school blocked out three days for this work to be accomplished. Every day, all day, students were free to work independently and in groups on their research. Teachers observed, made notes, and scored student performance on process as well as product. Although it was very difficult for teachers to be present and not help struggling students, the design provided a rare opportunity to see what students do when they are given a task with clear expectations but no other guidance. To the teachers' surprise, students stepped up to the task and most were fully engaged. Students were asked to describe their performance from both a process and a product perspective. Teachers were able to see how many of the self-directed behaviors were evidenced. This is the true test of the self-directed learner—observing what the student does when the "nag" factor disappears! Ultimately, that is the goal—for students to have developed strong enough habits for producing quality that they do their work without constant reminders.[2]

Modeling

Students watch to see if you are "walking the talk." They want to know that the habits that you are trying to develop in them are ones that you find useful in your experience. You can start by paying attention to your language, attitude, and application of the behaviors you are suggesting for students. As you think about your teaching, you might wonder aloud:

> Don't worry that children never listen to you; worry that they are always watching you.
>
> —Robert Fulghum

- "If I could do yesterday's lesson over, I'd read you more examples of good descriptions."
- "This week my goal is to finish my photo essay and share it with you."
- "I think this worked well because we read tons of news articles before trying to write one on our own."

You might ask,

"How might I improve this unit? What suggestions do you have for me to work on for the next time I teach this unit?"

"The class seems to be having a hard time learning this. How might I approach it to be more helpful? What are the problems, as you see them?"

A teacher at Furr High School in Houston, Texas, chooses a student from his English class to serve as a teaching assistant. He realizes that since he is a white, middle-class person teaching in a poor urban school, there is much to learn about the diverse population he teaches. His teaching assistant reviews his lessons to make certain that they are understandable and that they pay attention to the ethnic and racial diversity of his students. He asks for examples from the perspective of an adolescent so that he can provide meaningful analogies.

The process of self-assessment provides internal and external data that promote one's own learning and growth. Teachers can provide opportunities for developing and reflecting on such data. Providing opportunities for reflection models the value you place on this behavior.

Summary

Self-directed people consciously reflect upon, conceptualize, and apply understandings from one experience to another. As a result of this analysis and reflection, they synthesize new knowledge, learning accumulates, and concepts are derived and constructed. Confronting and solving problems becomes more routinized, particularized, and refined. Increasingly, self-directed people are capable of predicting consequences of their decisions and experiment more and take more risks. They expand their repertoire of techniques and strategies to use in different settings with varying contexts and unique situations. They ask themselves, "How can I continue to learn from these experiences?"

Notes

1. Adapted from Levy (1996). *Starting from Scratch: One Classroom Builds Its Own Curriculum.* Portsmouth, NH: Heinemann.

2. Appreciation for stimulating many of these ideas is expressed to William Baker, Pat Forte, and Peggy Luidens in their unpublished paper, "Promoting Self-Directed Learning with Students: Assisting Students to Reflect, Create Their Own Feedback, and Hone Capabilities of Self-Directedness" (Draft 7; February 2003).

CHAPTER 6

Adapting the Assessment Strategies for Your School and Classroom

Shifting the school culture away from an overly controlling environment to an environment that promotes self-directed learning will require changes at every level of the organization—from classroom to building to parents to central administration to Board of Education. The greater the consistency of expectation that students can and will learn how to become self-directed, responsible learners, the more likely students will demonstrate those behaviors in their performances. However, the shift is not an easy one. This chapter focuses on some ways to move the culture in this direction.

> It takes a village to raise a child.
>
> —African Proverb

The Place to Begin Is Within Yourself

Before we begin to develop self-awareness in others, we must become aware of our own values, standards, beliefs, and styles. As teachers expand their self-knowledge, they are more able to teach the way students learn best. With greater awareness of their own teaching and learning styles, many teachers discover that students who distress them the most are ones with cognitive styles different than their own.

For example, students who are abstract and random may drive a teacher whose own learning patterns are concrete and sequential to distraction. Self-awareness permits the teacher to set aside emotional responses to style differences in order to provide the best learning conditions for all students.

Instructional decisions of what and how to teach are informed by our beliefs and values. Self-knowledge includes self-awareness about our preferred learning styles, ethical considerations in teaching, assumptions and theories about learning, and professional mission and values. Deciding what and how to teach is informed by our beliefs and values. A math teacher, very clear about his own values, once said to us, "Its not about math, its about life."

Examining Your Own Beliefs and Assumptions About Self-Directed Learning

Because your beliefs strongly influence your decisions and actions, you are invited to examine some of your own beliefs that may be encouraging or inhibiting self-directed learning. Following are seven beliefs that merit your critical self-examination:

From External Evaluation to Self-Assessment. This entire book serves as an invitation to shift our perception of evaluation of learning from external to internal processes. Evaluation has been viewed as summative measures of how much content a student has retained. It is useful for grading and segregating students into ability groups.

Assessment should be neither summative nor punitive. Rather, assessment is a mechanism for providing ongoing feedback to the learner and to the organization as a necessary part of the spiraling processes of continuous renewal: self-managing, self-monitoring, and self-modifying. We must constantly remind ourselves that the ultimate purpose of evaluation is to have students learn to become self-evaluative. If students graduate from our schools still dependent upon others to tell them when they are adequate, good, or excellent, then we've missed the whole point of what self-directed learning is about.

Evaluation, the highest level of Bloom's Taxonomy (1956), means generating, holding in your head, and applying a set of internal and external criteria. For too long, adults alone have been practicing that skill. We need to shift that responsibility to students—to help them develop the capacity for self-analysis, self-referencing, and self-modification.

Examining Our Beliefs About Intelligence From Innate Capacity to Effort-Based Learning. Some teachers still embrace the idea that intelligence is inherited through the genes and chromosomes and that it can be measured by one's ability to score sufficiently on a test that yields a static and relatively stable IQ score.

There is an increasing body of research about the relationship between effort and ability.[1] When people view their intelligence as a fixed and unchangeable entity, they strive to obtain positive evaluations of their ability and to avoid displaying evidence of inadequate ability relative to others. A student's "intelligence" is demonstrated in task performance—he or she either has or lacks ability. This negative self-concept influences effort. Effort and ability are negatively related in determining achievement—having to expend great effort is taken as a sign of low ability.

Changing our conception of intelligence is one of the most liberating and powerful forces in our thinking. When we think of intelligence as something that grows incrementally, students tend to invest energy to learn something new or to increase their understanding and mastery of tasks. They display continued high levels of task-related effort in response to difficulty. Learning goals are associated with the inference that effort and ability are positively related, so that greater efforts create and make evident more ability.

Children develop cognitive strategies and effort-based beliefs about their intelligence—the habits of mind associated with higher-order learning—when they are continually pressed to raise questions and to accept challenges, to find solutions that are not immediately apparent, to explain concepts, justify their reasoning, and seek information. When we hold children accountable for this kind of intelligent behavior, they take it as a signal that we think they are smart, and they come to accept this judgment. The paradox is that children become smart by being treated as if they already are intelligent (Resnick, 2001).

Changing Our Beliefs About Meaning-Making. We discussed in Chapter 3 that meaning making is not a spectator sport. Knowledge is a constructive process rather than a finding. It is not the content stored in memory but the activity of constructing it that gets stored. Humans don't *get* ideas; they *make* ideas. Meaning making is not just an individual operation. The individual interacts with others to construct shared knowledge. There is a cycle of internalization of what is socially constructed as shared meaning, which is then externalized to affect the learner's social participation.

Our perceptions of learning need to shift from educational outcomes that are primarily an individual's collections of subskills to include

> The brain's capacity and desire to make or elicit patterns of meaning is one of the keys of brain-based learning. We never really understand something until we can create a model or metaphor derived from our unique personal world. The reality we perceive, feel, see and hear is influenced by the constructive processes of the brain as well as by the cues that impinge upon it.
>
> —Merlin C. Wittrock, *Handbook of Research on Teaching*

successful participation in socially organized activities and the development of students' identities as conscious, flexible, efficacious, and interdependent meaning makers. We assume that if we taught academic subjects and if students were to learn and be evaluated on how well they learn the minute subskills in each content area, they will somehow become the kind of people we want them to become (Seiger-Eherenberg, 1991).

We must let go of having learners acquire OUR meanings and have faith in the processes of individuals' construction of their own and shared meanings through individual activity and social interaction. That's scary, because the individual and the group may NOT construct the meaning we want them to: a real challenge to the basic educational framework with which most schools are comfortable.

Shifting Our Orientation From Compartmentalized Subjects to Transdisciplinary Learning. Our view of curriculum organized around separate disciplines limits teachers of different departments, grade levels, and disciplines meeting together, communicating about, and finding connections and continuities among students' learnings.

The disciplines as we have known them, however, may no longer exist. With the advent of increased technology and the pursuit of knowledge in all quarters of human endeavor, the separate disciplines are being replaced by human activities that draw upon vast, generalized, and transdisciplinary bodies of knowledge and relationships applied to unique, domain-specific settings. To be an archeologist today, for example, requires employment of radar and distant satellite infrared photography as well as an understanding radioactive isotopes. Professions have combined multiple disciplines into unique and ever-smaller specialties: Space-biology, genetic-technology, neuro-chemistry, astro-hydrology.

Separating the disciplines produces episodic, compartmentalized, and encapsulated thinking that inhibits transfer. When the biology teacher says, "Today we're going to learn to spell some biological terms," students often respond by saying, "Spelling—in biology? No way!" Biology has little meaning for physical education, which has no application to literature and has even less connection to algebra. They may be viewed as a series of subjects to be mastered rather than habituating the search for meaningful relationships and the application of knowledge beyond the context in which it was learned.

If students are to draw forth information from their storehouse of knowledge and apply it in new and novel situations, the curriculum should capitalize on the natural interdependency and interrelatedness of knowledge. Peter Senge (1997) contends that we are all natural systems thinkers, and the findings in cognitive research are compatible and supportive of the need to move from individual to collective intelligence, from disciplines to themes, from independence to relationships.

Shifting Our Paradigm From Knowing Right Answers to Knowing How to Behave When Answers Are Not Readily Apparent. Some teachers tend to teach, assess, and reward convergent thinking and the acquisition of content with a limited range of acceptable answers. Life in the real world, however, demands multiple ways to do something well. A fundamental shift is required from valuing right answers as the purpose for learning, to knowing how to behave when we *don't* know answers—knowing what to do when confronted with those paradoxical, dichotomous, enigmatic, confusing, ambiguous, discrepant, and sometimes overwhelming situations that plague our lives. An imperative mind-shift is essential—from valuing knowledge *acquisition* as an outcome to valuing knowledge *production* as an outcome. We want students to learn how to develop a critical stance with their work: inquiring, thinking flexibly, learning from another person's perspective. The critical attribute of intelligent human beings is not only having information, but knowing how to act on it.

As our paradigm shifts, we will need to let go of our obsession with acquiring content knowledge as an end in itself, and make room for viewing content as a vehicle for developing broader, more pervasive and complex goals such as personal efficacy, flexibility, craftsmanship, consciousness, and interdependence (Costa & Garmston, 2002).

Our curriculum must focus on such processes as learning to learn, knowledge production, metacognition, transference, decision making, creativity, and group problem solving. These *are* the subject matters of instruction. Content, selectively abandoned and judiciously chosen for its rich contributions to the thinking/learning process, becomes the vehicle to carry the learning. The focus is on learning FROM the objectives instead of learning OF the objectives (Costa & Leibmann, 1997a).

Altering Our Perspective From Uniformity to Diversity. In simpler times, when citizens seldom ventured farther than a horseback ride from home, our perception of a learning community was one in which all people thought and acted in a similar fashion. In 1847 the first graded school was invented in the United States. Believing that all children were pretty much alike, students were grouped by age and assigned to a grade. Content was allocated to and expected to be taught in each grade level and, by the end of each academic year, students were expected to have mastered that content. Today we perpetuate this fable of uniformity with "one size fits all" schools, as if all students can master content and skills on the same day and that they can demonstrate their learning in the same way (Eisner, 1999).

Human beings, however, are made to be different. Diversity is the basis of biological survival. Each of us has a unique genetic structure, exclusive facial features, distinguishing fingerprints, a distinctive signature, a diverse background of experience and culture, and a preferred way of learning and expressing our information and knowledge. We even have a singular frequency in which we vibrate (Leonard, 1978). We know that human development proceeds at a variable rate and that divergence is obvious in the styles, perceptual abilities, and intelligences with which we gather and process information to make meaning of our environment.

Each of us came for a purpose unique to who we are and appropriate to the overall mosaic of life. It is time we value the individual for his or her natural skills and talents instead of trying to create clones, all possessing the same abilities. Our old perceptions of uniformity need to yield in deference to valuing diversity—the true source of power in today's world.

Re-examining Our Assumptions, From Motivating Others to Learn to Liberating Their Innate Passion for Learning. Human beings are active, dynamic, self-organizing systems with an integration of mind, body, and spirit. One of the purest examples of a self-organizing learning system that integrates into greater levels of complexity is the young child. Infants and toddlers are in a constant state of exploring everything they can lay their hands, eyes, and lips on. They live in a state of continuous discovery: dismayed by anomaly, attracted to novelty, compelled to mastery, intrigued by mystery, curious about discrepancy. They derive personal and concrete feedback from their tactile/kinesthetic adventures. Their brains are actually being transformed with each new experience.

Unfortunately, training in mental and emotional passivity starts with the first days of school. Traditional school learning may cause students to perceive that the purpose of acquiring knowledge is to pass tests on the content, rather than accumulate wisdom and personal meaning from the content. Students learn to read someone else's static accounts of history, study abstract theories of science, and comprehend complex ideas unrelated to their own life experiences and personal aspirations. They perceive learning to be a game of mental gymnastics with little or no relevant application beyond the school to everyday living, further inquiry, or knowledge production.

The journey toward self-directed learning begins with a highly personal intellectual, psychological, and spiritual shift of consciousness that each of us must make if we want to educate children to think for themselves. The vision you hold for yourself as an educator may need to shift from that of information provider to being a catalyst, model, coach, innovator, researcher, and collaborator with the learner throughout the learning process in order to assist learners in becoming their own coach, catalyst, and researcher. Mind-shifts do not come easily, as they require letting go of old habits, old beliefs, and old traditions. There is a necessary disruption when we shift mental models. If there is not, we are probably not shifting; we may be following new recipes but we will end up with the same stew! Growth and change are found in "disequilibrium," not balance. Out of chaos, order is built, learning takes place, understandings are constructed, and gradually, organizations function more consistently as their vision is clarified, as their mission is forged, and their goals operationalized. In the words of Sylvia Robinson, "some people think you are strong when you hold on. Others think it is when you let go."

Getting Started in the Classroom

The Student as Resource Manager

Our traditional texts, workbooks, and notebooks are going the way of the typewriter, slide rule, and adding machine. Students today are growing up with, living in, and expect to learn through technological means. With the increase in technology, students will increasingly develop their own resources. They will access, select, synthesize, and manage the information that is available through a multitude of avenues and present it in unique, self-designed forms. Their understandings are being built from vast databases, more accessible than the reference books or encyclopedias of the past. They are in instantaneous, live communication with vast, worldwide resources previously unavailable to them.

As a result, the criteria for performance and learning must be a collaborative process. Ultimately, it is the student who, in the final analysis, determines what should be learned, how it should be learned, and whether it has been mastered or not. Relevant goals and outcomes emerge from within the student. If the student feels that the goals imposed from the outside are irrelevant, uninteresting, too complex, or to distant, little commitment will be made to learning them. If the strategy of learning is not vibrant in terms of the student's readiness, learning style, culture, and duration for mastery, little engagement will be exacted. Finally, if the form of assessment is not relevant to the student's capacity for the expression of his or her knowledge, little energy will be given to the acquisition of lasting proficiency.

Technology can become a significant tool, not only to enhance learning efficiency; it can also be a motivator for student engagement. The use of technology provides a means for planning, time management, and record keeping. Using the tools helps to involve students in participating in the construction of their own curriculum, having to decide what learning is of greatest worth as well as when and how it should be learned. One of the most significant features of the use of technology is that it provides immediate feedback about the student's learning progress.

Getting Started: A Vignette From a Second-Grade Classroom

THE ANT FARM

Our class has also written a class book entitled "The Ant Farm." It all started with author studies! The students were learning about various authors and one little girl suggested putting together a book. I told my principal in passing about this and she told me of another class that had a done a class book in the style of Eric Carle. I shared this example with my class and they decided to create their own story and illustrate it in the style of Barbara Reid using plasticine. At this point I was feeling very overwhelmed—how would we start such a project, how would it all come together, could we do it.

Basically—it felt a little out of control and I didn't know what the outcome would be. The students decided to write a story about an ant farm—as they had also been studying "Small Crawling and Flying Animals." It quickly escalated into a story about a little boy who is afraid of ants and who gets turned into an ant when his class begins studying ants in Science. They planned the story using a strategy called "Somebody Wanted But So (SWBS)"—to come up with a main character, a goal, a problem and a solution. The students told the story and I wrote it down. They created the characters, the setting, the details—they did all the planning and worked together as a class to create a story that is interesting and complete. It was amazing to see them take ownership—I heard comments such as "wait a minute—that doesn't follow our plan," as they worked out details in putting the story together. They thought back to what they had learned in their Science unit and to the criteria important in writing an effective story. They began to consider themselves authors as well as illustrators. They planned, edited, processed on the computer and then began sketching their illustrations.

(Continued)

(Continued)

This project most definitely was not mine—it was all them! After studying Barbara Reid's techniques they applied those techniques and began to transfer their sketches to plasticine illustrations. The work they produced was amazing—and it was completely evident that it belonged to them. They worked enthusiastically and carefully on their illustrations to ensure they closely resemble the sketches they had made and were careful to follow the process Barbara Reid went through. When doing the writing—they articulated the importance of editing and:

1. Making sure the story made sense and was interesting to read

2. Using capitals where they belong

3. Using correct spelling

The students paid close attention to the details of including a title page, dedication page, about the book, about the author and what was so great to see is how they could articulate the process they went through from start to finish and the ownership they felt about this project.

Was it out of my comfort zone? Initially—yes, but the thing about self-directed learning is when the students take off—you as the teacher are there to guide and help—but in many instances—you're along for the ride—learning as you go!

— Heather Weiler, second-grade teacher,
Glenora School, Edmonton, Canada

Getting Started in the Secondary School

Holding students responsible for their learning progress is a major mind-shift for many teachers. We frequently hear people say, "If only Ms. Smith would change . . ." or "Teachers need to . . ." or "If we had different students we might try . . ."Real change, however, begins with the individual. It all begins with you. Even if it is only one teacher at a time making the changes, the potential for contagion is greater when there is *at least* one teacher showing what is possible. Barbie Hansen, Alta Sierra Intermediate School, and Keith Whelan,

Category   Category

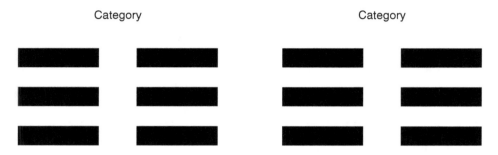

Figure 6.1   Example of an Affinity Chart

Buchanan High School in Clovis Unified School District, describe their movement to a self-directed learning classroom focused on continuous improvement of performance. Their notes on how they get started follow:

Day One: Expectations. I start setting the culture of the classroom the first day that the students enter my room. I greet them at the door and shake hands. Begin the session with brainstorming a list of student expectations, what do they expect of the teacher and the class. Give each student two Post-it notes. Use an affinity chart [see Figure 6.1] to compile the list. Discuss the responses. (Expectations are both operational and strategic. Guide the students to both.) Have a list of expectations from the teacher on chart paper. Go over the expectations for the students.

Affinity: Relationship or similarity; items that fall into the same category or classification have an *affinity* for each other.

Day Two: Jobs and Responsibilities: My Job, Your Job, Shared Responsibilities. Gave each student two Post-it notes. Have them write what they see as the #1 most important job or responsibility of the student on one Post-it note and the #1 most important job responsibility of the teacher on the second Post-it. Have an affinity chart on the board with three columns. The first column is the brainstorm answers to the question—What is your (the student's) job? And the second column is to brainstorm answers to the question—What is my (the teacher's) job?

Review the chart and ask if each entry is a shared job—one that is done together—and circle those that are shared. Add the shared responsibilities to the center column of the chart.

Table 6.1   Responsibility Chart

Student's Job/Responsibility	Shared	Teacher's Job/Responsibility

Day Three: Ground Rules. Create ground rules. Use affinity process to create ground rules with the students in your class. Give each student two sticky notes with the instruction to write the rules that are most important to the classroom. The teacher writes two on sticky notes also. The teacher facilitates the affinity process by choosing students to assist in placing them according to any affinity on a chart. After all notes are placed on the chart, each group of notes will form a positive guideline or ground rule. These are then written on the chart under the notes. This gives students a feeling of input into the operations of the class, creates greater buy-in and self-monitoring behavior.

Day Four: Goal Setting. Students do a self-evaluation of their strengths and weaknesses. They set goals for the six-week grading period. The student revisits these goals every six weeks. The students use the PDSA (plan, do, study, act) worksheet to reflect on what they have done to achieve their goals and set a new goal for the upcoming grading period.

Day Five: Class Goals. Use the affinity process to have the students input on a class grade goal. Come to a consensus on a common goal. I guide the students to set high standards for the class. We talk about how if they are doing their job, they should have a B– or above. We discuss solutions for missing assignments. The class grade goal is put on the chart.

From the Classroom to the Building

Although there are often powerful, individual practices in a building, agreement on practices for all teachers is a critical determinant for success. When one teacher requires students to become more self-evaluative and the next teacher does not, students are left trying to understand the procedures of each teacher rather than understanding themselves. We constantly hear the complaint that students are not demonstrating responsibility for their learning and, at the same time, we hear teachers talking about the amount of control they have over student work.

In Glenora School, they explicitly created an instructional focus for their building that they refer to as the "think back/look ahead" goal. The goal is stated in this way:

"All Glenora School students will enhance their higher level thinking skill of evaluation."

External Measure

By June 30, 2002, of our students who write the Provincial Achievement tests, 100% will achieve the acceptable standard on the skill reporting category of the math, science and social studies tests. As well, the percent of students achieving the standard of excellence in the skills reporting category will equal or surpass the percent of students achieving the standard of excellence in the knowledge reporting category.

Internal Measure

By June 30, 2002, 100% of students in kindergarten to grade two will be able to orally justify and make connections (give reasons and think back) when evaluating using the school developed criteria checklist. 100% of students in grades three to six will be able to justify, make connections and look ahead (apply their evaluations to new learning situations) using the school developed criteria checklist.

The goals are stated with explicit targets for performance. The faculty explored the question, "What behaviors, products, or performances would a student demonstrate who is an excellent 'evaluator'?" Based on charts from this session, they clarified their thinking. Finally, after much consideration, they developed a scope and sequence for curriculum and a scoring rubric for judgments about student performance. An excerpt from the scope and sequence follows.

Kindergarten—Grade Two

The students will be able to:

- Make a judgment
- Give at least one reason to support their judgment
- Stated reason(s) are logical, based on personal past experiences as well as careful observations
- Reason(s) consistently fit the topic

Or, for Grades Five and Six:

In addition to the skill achieved by the end of grade four, the students will be able to:

- State reasons that are based on criteria for success
- Reasons demonstrate meta-cognition
- Reasons are honest and objective
- Application of judgments or evaluations are based on the reasons the student has stated
- Students will demonstrate ability to anticipate a rebuttal and refute it

This example shows that there is (a) an explicitly stated goal for the school, (b) explicit curriculum designed developmentally, and (c) explicit ways to measure whether the students in the building are meeting the goals. When there is such a clear focus on evaluation, particularly self-evaluation, results are certain to follow.

A System Focus

Imagine the possibility that each building in the system were as clear about such expectations. If that were the case, students would know that self-directed learning, specifically as evidenced in students' becoming increasingly more self-evaluative, was expected, instructed, and assessed. Feedback about those behaviors would be a regular part of the reporting system. Report cards would include a component for students to provide self-reports. A summary of evidence from each building would be presented to the Board of Education and the community. Staff development would provide support for instruction and data analysis regarding the goals. Coaching support would be available in each building. In fact, all of the system structures and supports would focus on both the external and internal measures that lead to higher performance from students. The Board of Education would adopt these goals and accompany the goals with appropriate policies that support the education community to reach the goals.

Parental Support

Parents must be included in the enterprise. When students bring work home, parents must be able to understand the significance of the work and learn ways to support their child's efforts. They must learn how to make observations and ask their child to make observations rather than offering judgments. They need to learn how to ask good questions of their child about the work, such as the following:

1. I see you are working on number facts here. Help me understand what you have learned about the numbers.

2. I see that you have written an essay comparing two forms of government. Show me where you provided evidence for your opinions.

3. Your artwork is richer. You are using the space with greater variety. Did you have something specific in mind as you were working on this piece? Do you see a way to continue your work?

In Hommocks Middle School, Mamaroneck, New York, Lorraine McCurdy-Little sends the students' portfolios home to parents. Students are expected to walk through the portfolio with their parents. After the walk-through, parents respond to the student's writing.

The following are sample questions from Ms. McCurdy-Little and the parent's response:

Teacher: What questions do you have when you look through the pieces in this portfolio?

Parent: Amenda's writing always seems to come from the heart. Her soul searching came through as passion in her writing.

Teacher: What kind of conversation was inspired by your reading between you and your child?

Parent: We covered many moral and social issues. Amenda's interest in discovering her own opinions and prejudice has led to important opportunities to exchange our views with hers.

A special touch in this class is that the students are also asked, in the fourth quarter, to choose a teacher they had previously and send the portfolio to that teacher for a response. How satisfying for teachers from former years to observe the growth of a student they once had and to have the opportunity to respond to the student once again!

Ninety Ways to Bring Self-Directed Learning to Life

Following are numerous suggestions for ways to further the awareness of self-directed learning in your classrooms, school, and community. You will find this list purposefully incomplete. The reason, as you might infer, is to invite your staff, community, and students to brainstorm their own additions to the list to fit your situation.

While some ideas may not work for your particular setting, others may be of great relevance. Your team, group, or staff may wish to rank each item according to the following A, P, M, N Scale:

A = Already doing it
P = Priority: Implement immediately
M = Maybe—It might work
N = No way—It won't fly!

After ranking, develop an action plan to implement the P's; appoint a subcommittee to study the M's, and congratulate yourselves for already doing the A's!

1. Develop a self-directed learning Code of Ethics. Distribute it to every member of the school community. Refer to it often. Display it prominently. All school policies should reflect the implicit Code of Ethics.

2. Institute a student-to-student tutoring program around self-directed learning.

3. Promote a schoolwide or intraclass service club whose real mission is to infuse self-directed learning in the school, class, or external community.

4. Ensure that the school's recognition and reward systems are based on self-directed learning.

5. Use morning announcements, school/classroom bulletin boards, and/or the school newsletter to highlight the various self-directed accomplishments of students and faculty.

6. When conflicts arise around the school or class, draw upon dispositions of self-directed learning as ways to resolve and learn from the conflict.

7. Invite student volunteers to clean up their community, build a playground, pick up litter, plant tees, paint a mural, remove graffiti, or clean up a local park or beach. Which of the dispositions of self-directed learners do they draw upon?

8. Have students investigate the significance of the school's traditions. Which traditions emphasize self-directed learning?

9. Hold an orientation ceremony at the beginning and at the end of the school year to acquaint staff, students, and parents

with the school's recognition of and emphasis on self-directed learning.

10. In physical education and sports programs, place a premium on good sportsmanship. How are sportsmanship and self-directed learning related? How does participation in sports contribute to self-directed learning in life beyond sports?

11. Hang pictures of heroes and heroines in classrooms and halls. Include explanatory stories and texts about their demonstration of the dispositions of self-directed learning.

12. Take a walk through your school with your students, staff, parents, or school officials. Ask them to interpret the school's values from their observations of the school environment and interactions.

13. Interview students from a variety of grade levels. Ask, "What does it take to be successful in this school?" Compare what they report with the list of dispositions of self-directed learners.

14. Start a school scrapbook with photos, news stories, and memorabilia reflecting the school's history and accomplishments in self-directed learning. Involve school members in contributing to and maintaining the collection. Show it off to visitors and new families.

15. Publicly recognize self-directed learning in the work of the school's "unsung heroes" who keep the school running: The custodians, repairmen, secretaries, cafeteria workers, and volunteers.

16. Develop a system of welcoming and orienting new students to self-directed learning as a valued goal of your school.

17. Invite students to take responsibility for maintenance and beautification of the school. A class might "adopt a hallway," shelve misplaced books, plant flowers, post signs identifying the caretakers. Discuss what dispositions of self-directed learning are required.

18. Have students make a major report on a living public figure ("My Personal Hero") focusing on that person's dispositions of self-directed learning.

19. Insist that accuracy and precision matter. Homework should be handed in on time, neat, complete, and accurate.

20. Include the study of "local heroes" in social studies. What attributes of self-directedness make them heroes?

21. When forming cooperative learning groups, review the dispositions of self-directed learners and select one to become the focus of the group work. Toward the end of the work time, stop and reflect on the performance of those dispositions by individuals and by the group and on the effect their performance had on the group's interaction and productivity.

22. Celebrate the birthdays of heroes and heroines with a discussion of how self-directed learning contributed to their accomplishments.

23. Build empathy into literature and social studies by inviting students to "put themselves in the shoes" of the people they are reading about or studying.

24. Read and discuss biographies from all subject areas. Help students identify the person's core or defining characteristics. How do they compare with the dispositions of self-directed learning?

25. Invite students to write thoughtful letters: thank you notes, letters to public officials, letters to the editor, and so on, explaining how they use the attributes of self-directedness.

26. Set up a buddy reading system between an older and a younger class. Teach the older students techniques and dispositions (using clear and precise language, empathy, managing impulsivity, etc.) that will help make their teaching experience successful. Teach them how to draw upon dispositions of self-directed learning when they interpret the story and the characters.

27. Have students memorize poetry and important prose, such as the Preamble to the Constitution or the Gettysburg Address. Have them translate the ideas into terms that use the vocabulary of self-directed learning.

28. In math and science classes, specifically address such dispositions as applying previous knowledge, persistence, striving for accuracy and precision, or thinking and communicating with clarity and precision. Why are these essential to being successful in math or science? How are they applicable beyond math in other subject areas, in school, work, and in life?

29. Have students and staff discuss how class rules, school rules, discipline, and homework policies reflect and support self-directed learning.

30. In social studies, examine and reexamine, yearly, the responsibilities of the citizen. What can students and staff do now to build self-directed learning of responsible citizenship?

31. Have each staff member choose a personal motto or mission statement. Share it with students and explain why it was chosen.

32. Tell students who your heroes are and why you chose them.

33. Make your classroom expectations of self-directed learning clear and hold students accountable for meeting them.

34. Admit your mistakes to your students and how you seek to learn from them. Expect and encourage students to do the same.

35. Describe to students how you engage in self-directed learning outside of the classroom in community service, church work, hobbies, avocations, sports, and more.

36. Illustrate integrity; let your students see that you live the same expectations of self-directed learning that you place upon them.

37. Include in faculty/staff meetings and workshops discussions of the school's "ethos." How might self-directed learning become more apparent?

38. Develop a bulletin board where teachers, administrators, and students can share the awareness, use of, and growth in self-directed learning.

39. Notify parents of student performance of self-directed learning via notes, phone calls, personal visits, and so on.

40. Catch students being self-directed and write or call parents to report it.

41. Send a letter home to parents before the school year starts introducing yourself, your classroom, your enthusiasm, and your expectations of self-directedness in their children.

42. In the school newsletter, inform parents of the performance of students' self-directed learning.

43. Develop a list of suggested readings and resources in self-directed learning and share it with parents.

44. Include a "parents' corner" in the school newsletter where parents can share parenting tips, book titles, homework helps, and the like, all of which further self-directed learning.

45. Include anecdotes of commendable student performances in the school newsletter.

46. When a new student enrolls in the school, welcome the family as well.

47. During parent-teacher conferences, inquire into the parent's concerns. Model listening with understanding and empathy and use precise language.

48. Invite students to "adopt an elder" in the community. Arrange for students to visit, write letters, read to, and explain what is meant by self-directed learning to their adoptee.

49. Invite graduates of your school to return to talk about their experiences in the next stage of life. Ask them to discuss what dispositions of self-directed learning could make the transition from elementary to middle school, from middle school to high school, or from high school to work or college successful.

50. Invite managers and workers from industry and the corporate world to visit your school. Share with them the dispositions of self-directed learning and inquire about how these are being encouraged and used in their business.

51. During election years, encourage students to research a candidate's positions, listen to debates, participate in voter registration drives, and so on. Analyze the candidate's background and platform in terms of the dispositions of self-directed learning. What are indications of the candidate's integrity?

52. Organize a visit to a meeting of the City Council, Board of Supervisors, Board of Education, or other public decision-making body. Share with them that the students have been learning the dispositions of self-directed learning and that they wish to observe them in action in the meetings.

53. Interview parents about how they employ self-directed learning in their profession, job, or career and what dispositions make them successful.

54. Have students shadow school personnel—secretaries, custodians, cafeteria workers, the school nurse—to observe them for their self-directedness.

55. Prepare a videotape program to be shown to parents, new teachers, or district personnel illuminating what self-directed learning is and illustrating how self-directedness is being cultivated in your school and classrooms.

56. Set up your school-to-career program with an expectation that the students will learn about the use of self-directed learning in the workplace.

57. Ask the students in the computer labs to have a discussion about the use of self-directed learning as they are working with technology.

58. Create bulletin boards that focus on student work, with an analysis of how the dispositions of self-directed learning informed the work.

59. Provide bookmarks that have the dispositions of self-directed learners printed on them.

60. Make bumper stickers that celebrate the school's dedication to self-directed learning.

61. Have students develop their own buttons to recognize and reward use of the dispositions of self-directed learning.

62. Place a sign in the playground that suggests that students use the dispositions of self-directedness as they are playing with one another.

63. Study television programs, searching for examples of use of self-directed learning. In which programs do you find greatest evidence and value of self-directed learning?

64. Study great painters and consider how self-directed learning might influence their work.

65. Set up a metacognitive journal for the whole class in which students can record observations of indicators of self-directed learning.

66. Examine the pictures, icons, and heroes on the coins and currency of foreign countries. Discover why they qualify to be considered national icons and which of the dispositions of self-directed learning are being exemplified.

67. Develop a calendar for the school year designating one disposition to be emphasized per month or week. Suggest activities for parents and teachers to illuminate that disposition each week.

68. Take advantage of school holidays: Presidents' Day, Martin Luther King Day, Labor Day, and so on. Use the dispositions of self-directed learning to explain why these are important days to be commemorated.

69. Locate cartoons in the newspaper and magazines that illustrate one or more of the dispositions of self-directed learning. Make a display in the school or classroom. Discuss with students which dispositions each cartoon illustrates and why.

70. Write letters to businesses and corporations asking how they use the dispositions of self-directed learning.

71. Write a letter to the senior citizen group in your community and ask them to describe how these dispositions were used when they were younger.

72. Make a chart of the dispositions of self-directed learners and chart the growth of members of the class.

73. Interview community members and discover their perceptions of self-directed learning.

74. Create plays, poems, and dialogues in which self-directed learning is central.

75. Have your students create a way to communicate the meaning and need for self-directed learning for back-to-school night.

76. Place on the wall of your classroom large sheets of paper with magic markers attached nearby. Put the name of each of the dispositions of self-directed learning on a sheet. Have parents put associations to the dispositions on the sheets as they walk about the room.

77. Choose a few of the dispositions of self-directed learning to set as ground rules for discussions.

78. Create a quilting project and make a quilt for each of the dispositions similar to the ones made in colonial times for mottoes or aphorisms.

79. Design plaques and posters for the classroom for each of the dispositions of self-directed learning.

80. Create rap songs about self-directed learning.

81. Select and watch films to determine which self-directed learning the main characters exemplify (Babe: Listening with understanding and empathy; Chariots of Fire: Persisting; Dead Poet's Society: Thinking flexibly; It's a Wonderful Life: Persisting; Apollo 13: Imagining, creating, innovating).

82. _____

83. _____

84. _____

85. _____

86. _____

87. _____

88. _____

89. _____

90. _____

Summary

We leave you to complete this list and invent the next 99 ways to get started. Bring a committee together. Invite students to add to the list. Ask parents how they might get started at home. Getting started just requires the initiative and the energy to follow through. What is more difficult is sustaining what you start. Students are eager to participate in a reliable, consistent culture that assumes that they are capable of learning and provides the opportunities for self-direction in their learning. Are we ready to let them go?

> Put yourself in a state of mind where you say to yourself, "Here is an opportunity for me to celebrate like never before, my own power, my own ability to get myself to do whatever is necessary."
>
> —Tony Robbins

Note

1. For an additional discussion of this change in our understanding of intelligence, see Costa and Kallick (2002), Fogarty (2002, chap. 26), and Perkins (1995).

Afterword

Abraham Maslow (1968) introduced the notion of "self-actualization." He provided a powerful theory of the human need or drive for personal fulfillment and the need for evidence that "one is achieving fully what he or she is capable of becoming" (Covington, 1992). Maslow's theory suggests that human beings possess an innate drive, a built-in motivation to achieve their aspirations, to fulfill their potential, and to become increasingly successful. We share this belief.

Contrary to this belief, we are in an era in which successful performance is measured so much by "others" that we are in danger of students losing the belief that success is best measured from within. In a recent survey of eighteen states' practices that make extensive use of high-stakes testing, the "stakes" included the following (Amrein & Berliner, 2003):

- Graduation is contingent on the high school graduation exam.
- Grade-to-grade promotion is contingent on a promotion exam.
- The state publishes annual school or district report cards.
- The state identifies low-performing schools according to whether they meet state standards or improve year to year.
- Monetary awards are given to high-performing or improving schools.
- The state has authority to close, reconstitute, or revoke accreditation or take over low-performing schools.
- The state has authority to replace school personnel—principals or teachers—due to low test scores.
- The state permits students in failing schools to enroll elsewhere.

Absent from this list is any mention of how data are used to inform, energize, and contribute to the continuous learning of the student.

The intent of this book is to present an alternate point of view: that the major purpose of assessment is for students to assess themselves so that they can become more self-managing, self-monitoring, and self-modifying—to take control of themselves, to be responsible for their actions. We want them to be able to find ways to make learning meaningful and relevant to the actions they will take in their lives beyond school.

We must build a culture in schools that promotes these values. School systems must learn how to be systems and not just a collection of buildings in a common geographic area. As much as we claim that we are a community of learners, too often our need for individuality eclipses our possibility for community. When we talk about self-directed learning, we are not talking about learners who are self-centered. We are talking about learners who value the synergy of collaboration as much as they value the right to be unique. And we especially value the leaders who press us to think from the individual to the building to the district and out into the larger system in which schools reside.

Technology provides the opportunity for increased communication among schools and within the school communities. We can build communities of learning that start local and become international. For the first time in our history, we can be resources to one another without needing to have physical meetings. Our ideas intersect and gain momentum from our virtual meetings as much as our physical meetings. We can use the Internet, share videoconferences, and exchange publications as well as meet to enhance our relationships. It takes initiative to use technology to the greatest advantage. The more we are energized by our opportunities to learn, the more likely we will become lifelong learners.

The society in which we live requires independent, self-directed thinkers who appreciate diversity. The workplace needs such people, the political system needs such people, and the world needs such people. We are educating the caretakers of democracy. We must educate them to learn how to take action, take a stand, and volunteer for worthwhile causes. They must learn how to live in a world of highly diverse people and ideas.

> "Always bear in mind that your own resolution to succeed is more important than any other thing."
>
> —Abraham Lincoln, U.S. President

It all begins with you, the reader. You must embody your beliefs and principles in all that you do. You must be self-directed, even when the system in which you reside presents barriers. You are the leader. You must be able to take charge of the change. Try new ideas. Meet and share your successes and your concerns with others. Inspire study groups. Build networks. Live your dreams, and never forget why you entered the teaching profession. We shape the next generation of thinkers. Keep them thinking!

Quotations About Self-Directed Learning

Like metaphors, pithy quotations can deepen meanings with a few well-chosen words. This collection of quotations by authors, artists, philosophers, psychologists, businesspeople, athletes, scientists, statespeople, and historians is intended to accompany and illuminate the meaning of and necessity for self-directed learning. The purpose of this collection is to support anyone working on self-directed learning as an additional resource. Selected quotations may be

- made into banners or posters to mount in conspicuous places as reminders,
- studied to find what hidden meanings and relationships might be disclosed,
- highlighted in monthly calendars focusing on one of the intellectual dispositions,
- chosen as a topic to stimulate further writing and reflection,
- the focus of "words to live by" for an extended period of time,
- related to a topic of study in one or more content areas,
- used in other ways that you will create.

This is only the beginning. You will want to find other ways to use them as well as add to the collection.

◆

No power on earth can impede your progress as surely and implacably as you can.

— Colin Turner, Author
From the book, *Born to Succeed*

◆

It is of practical value to learn to like yourself. Since you must spend so much time with yourself you might as well get some satisfaction out of the relationship.

— Norman Vincent Peale

It's not what happens to you; it's what you do about it that makes the difference.

— W. Mitchell

The man who can drive himself further once the effort gets painful is the man who will win.

— Roger Bannister

We distinguish the excellent man from the common man by saying that the former is the one who makes great demands upon himself, and the latter makes no demands on himself.

— Jose Ortega y Gasset

The relationships we have with the world are largely determined by the relationships we have with ourselves.

— Greg Anderson

The self is not something that one finds. It is something one creates.

— Thomas Szasz

You are your own raw material. When you know what you consist of and what you want to make of it, then you can invent yourself.

— Warren B. Bennis

Spoon-feeding, in the long run, teaches us nothing but the shape of the spoon.

— E. M. Forester

Not everything that can be counted, counts. And not everything that counts can be counted.

— Albert Einstein

To be what we are, and to become what we are capable of becoming, is the only end of life.

— Robert Louis Stevenson

The abundant life does not come to those who have had a lot of obstacles removed from their path by others. It develops from within and is rooted in strong mental and moral fiber.

— William Mather Lewis,
Speaker and University President

Learn to depend upon yourself by doing things in accordance with your own way of thinking.

— Grenville Kleiser

There is only one corner of the universe you can be certain of improving and that's your own self.

— Aldous Huxley, Author

The circumstances in life, the events in life, the people around me in life do not make me the I am but reveal the way I am.

— Jim St. John

Reflection is turning a topic over in various aspects and in various lights so that nothing significant will be overlooked.

— John Dewey

He who knows others is wise; He who knows himself is enlightened.

— Lao-Tzu

The first person we have to tell the truth to is ourselves. If we are not going to be honest with ourselves, there is little possibility that we will treat anyone else differently.

— Toinette Lippe, Author,
Nothing Left Over: A Plain and Simple Life

If you don't run your own life, somebody else will.

— John Atkinson

Self-assurance is two thirds of success.

— Gaelic Proverb

You might well remember that nothing can bring you success but yourself. Embrace and love all of yourself—past, present, and future.
Forgive yourself quickly and as often as necessary.
Encourage yourself. Tell yourself good things about yourself.

— Melody Beattie, Author

Self-production: the characteristic of living systems to continuously renew themselves and to regulate this process in such a way that the integrity of their structure is maintained. It is a natural process which supports the quest for structure, process renewal and integrity.

— Margaret Wheatley

"I must do something" always solves more problems than "Something must be done."

— Anonymous

When a man points a finger at someone else, he should remember that four of his fingers are pointing at himself.

— Louis Nizer

If you want children to keep their feet on the ground, put some responsibility on their shoulders.

— Abigail Van Buren

Life isn't about finding yourself. Life is about creating yourself.

— George Bernard Shaw

◆

They always say time changes things, but you actually have to change them yourself.

— Andy Warhol

◆

There is no man so low that the cure for his condition does not lie strictly within himself.

— Thomas L. Masson

◆

If you want to succeed in the world, you must make your own opportunities.

— John B. Gough

◆

My future is one I must make myself.

— Louis L'Amour

◆

Teachers open the door, but you must enter by yourself.

— Chinese Proverb

◆

Every man is the architect of his own fortune.

— Sallust

◆

Greatness comes with recognizing that your potential is limited only by how you choose, how you use your freedom, how resolute you are, how persistent you are—in short, by your attitude.

— Peter Koestenbaum, Philosopher

◆

There is no dependence that can be sure but a dependence upon one's self.

— John Gay

◆

If you would have a faithful servant, and one that you like, serve yourself.

— Benjamin Franklin

◆

I have always regarded myself as the pillar of my life.

— Meryl Streep

◆

Use what talent you possess: The woods would be very silent if no birds sang except those that sang best.

— Henry Van Dyke

◆

The only person you should ever compete with is yourself. You can't hope for a fairer match.

— Todd Ruthman

◆

You have the power to declare the person you are becoming.

— Joe Marino

◆

You must have control of the authorship of your own destiny. The pen that writes your life story must be held in your own hand.

— Irene C. Kassorla

◆

It is not easy to find happiness in ourselves, and it is not possible to find it elsewhere.

— Agnes Repplier

◆

Self-reverence, self-knowledge, self-control. These three alone lead to sovereign power.

— Lord Tennyson

◆

God has entrusted me with myself.

— Epictetus

◆

Trust yourself. You know more than you think you do.

— Benjamin Spock

To the question of your life you are the answer, and to the problems of your life you are the solution.

— Joe Cordare

Perhaps for the first time in history, humankind has the capacity to create far more information than anyone can absorb; to foster far greater interdependency than anyone can manage, and to accelerate change far faster than anyone's ability to keep pace.

— Peter Senge

Only the human brain can deliberately change perceptions, change patterns, invent concepts and tolerate ambiguity.

— Edward de Bono

I hear people everywhere saying that the trouble with our time is that we have no great leaders any more. If we look back we always had them. But to me it seems there is a very profound reason why there are no great leaders any more. It is because they are no longer needed. The message is clear. You no longer want to be led from the outside. Every man must be his own leader. He now knows enough not to follow other people. He must follow the light that's within himself, and through this light he will create a new community.

— Laurens Van der Post

One of the purest examples of a self-organizing learning system which organizes into greater levels of complexity is the young child. Infants are in a constant state of exploration into everything they can lay their hands, eyes, and lips on. They live in a state of continuous discovery: Dismayed by anomaly, attracted to novelty, compelled to mastery, intrigued by mystery, curious about discrepancy. They derive personal and concrete feedback from their tactile/kinesthetic adventures. Their brains are actually being transformed with each new experience.

— Art Costa

A goal of education, therefore, is to assist growth toward greater complexity and integration and to assist in the process of self-organization—to modify individuals' capacity to modify themselves.

— Reuven Feuerstein, 1981

. . . a person and an organization must have goals, take actions to achieve those goals, gather evidence of achievement, study and reflect on the data and from that take action again. Thus, they are in a continuous feedback spiral toward continuous improvement.

— This is what W. Edwards Demming meant by *Kaizen*

Change your thoughts and you change your world.

— Norman Vincent Peale

The way in which we think of ourselves has everything to do with how our world sees us.

— Arlene Raven

Each human being is bred with a unique set of potentials that yearn to be fulfilled as surely as the acorn yearns to become the oak within it.

— Aristotle, Philosopher

Put yourself in a state of mind where you say to yourself, "Here is an opportunity for me to celebrate like never before, my own power, my own ability to get myself to do whatever is necessary."

— Tony Robbins

Success based on anything but internal fulfillment is bound to be empty.

— Martha Friedman

You are all you will ever have for certain.

— June Havoc

Nobody can give you wiser advice than yourself.

— Cicero

You are the only person on earth who can use your ability.

— Zig Ziglar

I know of no more encouraging fact than the unquestionable ability of man to elevate his life by conscious endeavor.

— Henry David Thoreau

If we did the things we are capable of, we would astound ourselves.

— Thomas A. Edison

He who joyfully marches to music in rank and file has already earned my contempt. He has been given a large brain by mistake, since for him the spinal cord would suffice.

— Albert Einstein

Avoid the crowd. Do your own thinking independently. Be the chess player, not the chess piece.

— Ralph Charell

For most men life is a search for the proper manila envelope in which to get themselves filed.

— Clifton Fadiman

Cherish that which is within you, and shut off that which is without; for much knowledge is a curse.

— Chuang-tzu

Our remedies oft in ourselves do lie, which we ascribe to Heaven.

— Shakespeare

Use your own best judgment at all times.

— Nordstrom's Department Store manual

Always bear in mind that your own resolution to succeed is more important than any other thing.

— Abraham Lincoln, U.S. President

Self-reliance is the only road to true freedom, and being one's own person is its ultimate reward.

— Patricia Sampson

You've got to find the force inside you.

— Joseph Campbell

The best helping hand that you will ever receive is the one at the end of your own arm.

— Fred Dehner

◆

The Wizard of Oz was right when he said to believe in ourselves. . . . Like Dorothy, we must be true to ourselves and allow others to help us reveal the answers that are already inside of us.

— Brian Koslow

◆

By learning to be with myself, to bring peace to myself, I can be more effective both in creating happiness in my own life and in offering a helping hand to others.

— Ingrid Bacci, Author

◆

Maturity involves being honest and true to oneself, making decisions based on a conscious internal process, assuming responsibility for one's decisions . . .

— Mary Pipher, Clinical Psychologist

◆

The only prison we need to escape from is the prison of our own minds.

— Anonymous

How things look on the outside of us depends on how things are on the inside of us.

— Park Cousins

Clear your mind of "can't."

— Samuel Johnson

There can be no progress (real, that is, moral) except in the individual and by the individual himself.

— Charles Baudelaire, French poet

If you don't like how things are, change it! You're not a tree. You have the ability to totally transform every area in your life—and it all begins with your very own power of choice.

— Jim Rohn, Author and Speaker

When I let go of what I am, I become what I might be.

— Lao Tzu

♦

You have to expect things of yourself before you can do them.

— Michael Jordan, Basketball Player

♦

The real person you are is revealed in the moments when you're certain no other person is watching. When no one is watching, you are driven by what you expect of yourself.

— Ralph S. Marston Jr.

♦

He who controls others is powerful but he who masters himself is more powerful still.

— Lao Tzu

♦

You don't just learn knowledge; you have to create it. Get in the driver's seat, don't just be a passenger. You have to contribute to it or you don't understand it.

— Dr. W. Edwards Deming

To have that sense of one's intrinsic worth which constitutes self-respect is potentially to have everything.

— Joan Didion

It never occurs to me that there are things that I can't do.

— Whoopi Goldberg, Actress

Learn to depend upon yourself by doing things in accordance with your own way of thinking.

— Grenville Kleiser

To decide to be at the level of choice is to take responsibility for your life and to be in control of your life.

— Arbie M. Dale, Author

My parents taught me that I could do anything I wanted and I have always believed it to be true. Add a clear idea of what inspires you, dedicate your energies to its pursuit and there is no knowing what you can achieve, particularly if others are inspired by your dream and offer their help.

— Pete Goss
(Sailor who successfully sailed around the world—alone)

Selected Resources to Support Self-Directed Learning

Selected Readings

Bandura, A. (1997). *Cognitive functioning in self-efficacy: The exercise of control* (pp. 212-258). New York: Freeman.

Brookfield, S. (Ed.). (1985). *Self-directed learning: From theory to practice* (New Directions for Continuing Education, Vol. 25). San Francisco: Jossey-Bass.

Brown, A. L. (1985). Motivation to learn and understand: On taking charge of one's own learning. *Cognition and Instruction, 5*(4), 311-322.

Brown, D. F. (2002). Self-directed learning in an 8th grade classroom. *Educational Leadership, 60*(1), 54-58.

Caffarella, R. S., O'Donnel, J. M. (1987). Self-directed learning: A critical paradigm revisited. *Adult Education Quarterly, 37*, 199-211.

Caine, G., & Caine, R. (2001). *The brain, education and the competitive edge.* Lanham, MD: Scarecrow Press.

Costa, A. (1991). The *school as a home for the mind.* Palatine, IL: Skylights.

Costa, A. (2001). *Developing minds: A resource book for teaching thinking.* Alexandria, VA: Association for Supervision and Curriculum Development.

Costa, A., & Garmston, R. (2002). *Cognitive coaching: A foundation for renaissance schools.* Norwood, MA: Christopher-Gordon.

Costa, A., & Kallick, B. (2000). *Discovering and exploring habits of mind* (Habits of Mind: A Developmental Series, Vol. 1). Alexandria, VA: Association for Supervision and Curriculum Development.

Costa, A., & Kallick, B. (2000). *Activating and engaging habits of mind* (Habits of Mind: A Developmental Series, Vol. 2). Alexandria, VA: Association for Supervision and Curriculum Development.

Costa, A., & Kallick, B. (2000). *Assessing and reporting habits of mind* (Habits of Mind: A Developmental Series, Vol. 3). Alexandria, VA: Association for Supervision and Curriculum Development.

Costa, A., & Kallick, B. (2000). *Integrating and sustaining habits of mind* (Habits of Mind: A Developmental Series, Vol. 4). Alexandria, VA: Association for Supervision and Curriculum Development.

Costa, A., & Liebmann, R. (1996). *Envisioning process as content: Toward a Renaissance curriculum.* Thousand Oaks, CA: Corwin Press.

Costa, A., & Liebmann, R. (1997). *The process centered school: Sustaining a Renaissance community.* Thousand Oaks, CA: Corwin Press.

Costa, A., & Liebmann, R. (1997). *Supporting the spirit of learning: When process is content.* Thousand Oaks, CA: Corwin Press.

Deci, E. (1995). *Why we do what we do.* New York: Grosset Putnam.

Della Doro, D. (1979). *Moving toward self-directed learning.* Alexandria, VA: Association for Supervision and Curriculum Development.

Ellison, J., & Hayes, C. (Eds.). (2003). *Cognitive coaching: Weaving threads of learning and change into the culture of the organization.* Norwood, MA: Christopher-Gordon.

Fogarty, R., Perkins, D., & Barell, J. (1992). *The mindful school: How to teach for transfer.* Palatine, IL: Skylights.

Garfield, C. (1986). *Peak performers: The new heroes of American business.* New York: William Morrow.

Garmston, R., & Wellman, B. (1999). *The adaptive school: A sourcebook for developing collaborative groups.* Norwood, MA: Christopher-Gordon.

Grow, G. O. (1991). Teaching learners to be self-directed. *Adult Education Quarterly, 41*(3), 125–149.

Hansen, J. (1998). *When learners evaluate.* Portsmouth, NH: Heinemann.

Kamii, C., Gones, S., & Joseph, L. (1991, April). When kids make their own math, they can make math their own. *Power Line, 1*(2), 1-2.

Knowles, M. S. (1975). *Self-directed learning: A guide for learners and teachers.* Englewood Cliffs, NJ: Prentice Hall.

Kohn, A. (1991, March). Teaching children to care. *Phi Delta Kappan, 72*(7), 497-506.

Kohn, A. (1994). Punished *by rewards: The trouble with gold stars, incentive plans, A's, praise and other bribes.* Boston: Houghton Mifflin.

Lipton, L., & Wellman, B., with C. Humbard. (2001). *Mentoring matters: A practical guide to learning-focused relationships.* Sherman, CT: LLC. (Available from www.MiraVia.com)

Long, H. B., & Associates. (Eds.). (1989). *Self-directed learning: Emerging theory and practice.* Norman: University of Oklahoma Research Center for Continuing Professional and Higher Education.

Oddi, L. F. (1986). Development and validation of an instrument to identify self-directed continuing learners. *Adult Education Quarterly, 36,* 97-107.

Pajares, F. (1996). Self-efficacy beliefs in academic settings. *Review of Educational Research, 66*(4), 543-578.

Perkins, D. (1992). *Smart schools: From training memories to educating minds.* New York: Free Press.

Perkins, D., Goodrich, H., Tishman, S., & Owen, J. (1993). *Thinking connections: Learning to think and thinking to learn.* Menlo Park, CA: Addison Wesley.

Preece, A. (1995). Self-evaluation: Making it matter. In A. Costa & B. Kallick (Eds.), *Assessment in the learning organization: Shifting the paradigm.* Alexandria, VA: Association for Supervision and Curriculum Development.

Sanford, C. (1995). *Myths of organizational effectiveness at work.* Battle Ground, WA: Springhill.

Stipek, D., & Seal, K. (2001). *Motivated minds: Raising children to love learning.* New York: Henry Holt.

Tishman, S., Perkins, D., & Jay, E. (1995). *The thinking classroom.* Boston: Allyn & Bacon.

Tschannen-Moran, M., Woolfolk Hoy, A., & Hoy, W. K. (1998). Teacher efficacy: Its meaning and measure. *Review of Educational Research, 68*(2), 202-248.

Tobin, D. A. (2000). *All learning is self-directed.* Alexandria, VA: American Society for Training and Development.

Wilson, J., & Leslie Wing J. (1993). *Thinking for themselves: Developing strategies for reflective learning.* New York: Heinemann.

York-Barr, J., Sommers, W., Ghere, G., & Montie, J. (2001*). Reflective practice to improve schools: An action guide for educators.* Thousand Oaks, CA: Corwin Press.

Video Productions

Costa, A., Kallick, B., & Leibowitz, M. (1996). *Self-directed learning.* Santa Monica, CA: Lee Canter Associates. (P.O. Box 2113, Santa Monica, CA 90407)

Costa, A., Kallick, B., & Leibowitz, M. (1996). *Habits of mind: Thinking skills that promote self-directed learning.* Santa Monica, CA: Lee Canter Associates. (P.O. Box 2113 Santa Monica CA 90407)

Costa, A. (1997). Teaching intelligent behaviors for thinking and problem solving. Salt Lake City, UT: The Video Journal of Education (http//www.videojurnal.com).

Costa, A. (1998). *Habits of mind: Dispositions of thinking.* Skylights Professional Development, 2626 Clearbrook Dr., Arlington Heights, IL 60005.

Costa, A. (1999). *Linking thinking and achievement in the classroom.* Skylights Professional Development, 2626 Clearbrook Dr., Arlington Heights, IL 60005.

Kallick, B. (1993). *Portfolio assessment.* Salt Lake City, UT: The Video Journal of Education.

Audio Productions

Costa, A. (1998). *Environments that mediate intellectual growth.* Skylights Professional Development, 2626 Clearbrook Dr., Arlington Heights, IL 60005.

Costa, A. (1999). *Changing curriculum means changing your mind.* Edmonton, Alberta, Canada: Kennedy Recordings, 537 Lessard Dr. 16M 1A9. Phone (780)-486-1335 (online at www.tgx.com/kennedy)

Costa, A. (1999*). Five passions: The sources of effective thinking.* Skylights Professional Development, 2626 Clearbrook Dr., Arlington Heights, IL 60005.

Costa, A. (1999). *Teaching and assessing habits of mind.* Edmonton, Alberta, Canada: Kennedy Recordings, 537 Lessard Dr. 16M 1A9. Phone (780)-486-1335 (online at www.tgx.com/kennedy)

Kallick, B. (1992). *Classroom assessment: New alternative.* Technology Pathways Corporation, 1304 West Street, Guilford, CT, 06437.

Kallick, B. (1992). *Collaborative Learning: Strategies to Encourage Thinking.* Technology Pathways Corporation, 1304 West Street, Guilford, CT, 06437.

Kallick, B (1992). *Creative and Critical Thinking: Teaching Strategies That Work.* Technology Pathways Corporation, 1304 West Street, Guilford, CT, 06437.

Computer Productions

Kallick, B., & Wilson, J. (1998). *Techpaths for math.* Guilford, CT. CD ROM-Math authentic assessment management system for grades K-8 with a database of over 100 authentic math tasks designed by math teachers. 203-457-1990 or e-mail: Carol@techpaths.com.

References

Amrein, A. L., & Berliner, D. C. (2003). The effects of high stakes testing on student motivation and learning. *Educational Leadership, 60*(5), 32-37.

Baker, B., Costa, A., & Shalit, S. (1997). Norms of collaboration: Attaining communicative competence. In A. Costa & R. Liebmann (Eds.), *The process centered school: Sustaining a renaissance community* (pp. 119-142). Thousand Oaks, CA: Corwin Press.

Bandura, A. (1997). *Self-efficacy: The exercise of control.* New York: Freeman.

Bloom, B. S. (Ed.), with M. D. Englehart, E. J. Furst, W. H Hill, & D. R. Krathwohl. (1956). *Taxonomy of educational objectives: Handbook 1. Cognitive domain.* New York: David McKay.

Bloom, B., & Krathwohl, D. (1956). *Taxonomy of educational objectives: Handbook I. Cognitive domain.* New York: David McKay.

Briggs, T. (1999, February 25). Passion for what they do keeps alumni on first team. *USA Today,* pp. 1A-2A.

Brooks, J. G., & Brooks, M. (2001). Becoming a constructivist teacher. In A. Costa (Ed.), *Developing minds: A resource book for teaching thinking.* Alexandria, VA: Association for Supervision and Curriculum Development.

Bruner, J. (1968). *The process of education.* Cambridge, MA: Harvard University Press.

California State Department of Education. (1997). *Standards for the teaching profession.* Sacramento, CA: Department of Education.

Costa, A. (2001). Habits of mind. In A. Costa (Ed.), *Developing minds: A resource book for teaching thinking.* Alexandria, VA: Association for Supervision and Curriculum Development.

Costa, A., & Garmston, R. (2002). *Cognitive coaching: A foundation for renaissance schools.* Norwood, MA: Christopher-Gordon.

Costa, A., & Kallick, B. (1994). *Assessment in the learning organization.* Alexandria, VA: Association for Supervision and Curriculum Development.

Costa, A., & Kallick, B. (2000). Habits of mind: Changing our perspectives about intelligence. In A. Costa & B. Kallick (Eds.), *Discovering and exploring habits of mind.* Alexandria VA: Association for Supervision and Curriculum Development.

Costa, A., & Kallick, B. (2000a). *Discovering and exploring habits of mind* (Habits of mind: A developmental series, Vol. 1). Alexandria, VA: Association for Supervision and Curriculum Development.

Costa, A., & Kallick, B. (2000b). *Activating and engaging habits of mind* (Habits of mind: A developmental series, Vol. 2). Alexandria, VA: Association for Supervision and Curriculum Development.

Costa, A., & Kallick, B. (2000c). *Assessing and reporting on growth of habits of mind* (Habits of mind: A developmental series, Vol. 3). Alexandria, VA: Association for Supervision and Curriculum Development.

Costa, A., & Kallick, B. (2000d). *Integrating and sustaining habits of mind* (Habits of mind: A developmental series, Vol. 4). Alexandria, VA: Association for Supervision and Curriculum Development.

Costa, A., & Liebmann, R. (1997a). *Process as content.* Thousand Oaks, CA: Corwin Press.

Costa, A., & Liebmann, R. (1997b). Towards a Renaissance curriculum: An idea whose time has come. In A. Costa & R. Liebmann (Eds.), *Envisioning process as content: Toward a Renaissance curriculum.* Thousand Oaks, CA: Corwin Press.

Covey, S. (1989). *Seven habits of highly effective people.* New York: Simon & Schuster.

Covington, M. V. (1992). *Making the grade: A self-work perspective on motivation and school reform.* New York: Cambridge University Press.

Danielson, C. (1996). *Enhancing professional practice: A framework for teaching.* Alexandria, VA: Association for Supervision and Curriculum Development.

Deci, E. (1995). *Why we do what we do.* New York: Grosset Putnam.

Dent, H. (1995). *Job shock: Four new principles of transforming our work and business.* New York: St. Martin's.

Dewey, J. (1938.) *Experience and education.* New York: Collier.

Education by design. (1998). Critical Skills Program, Antioch New England Graduate School, Keene, NH.

Eisner, E. (1999, May). The uses and limits of performance assessment. *Phi Delta Kappan, 80*(9), 658-660.

Feuerstein, R. (2000). Mediated learning experience. In A. Costa (Ed.), *Teaching for intelligence II: A collection of articles.* Arlington Heights, IL: Skylights.

Feuerstein, R., Rand, Y., Hoffman, M., & Miller, R. (1980). *Instrumental enrichment: An intervention program for cognitive modifiability.* Baltimore, MD: University Park Press.

Fogarty, R. (2002). Our changing perspective of intelligence: Master architects of the intellect. In A. Costa (Ed.), *Developing minds: A resource book for teaching thinking.* Alexandria, VA: Association for Supervision and Curriculum Development.

Garfield, C. (1995). *Peak performers: The new heroes of American business.* New York: William Morrow.

Garmston, R., & Garmston, S. (2002, November). *Using teaching standards for self-directed learning.* Paper presented at the Administrators Conference of the East Asian Region Council of Overseas Schools, Beijing, China.

Garmston, R., & Wellman, B. (1999). *The adaptive school: A sourcebook for developing collaborative groups.* Norwood, MA: Christopher-Gordon.

Goleman, D. (1995). *Emotional intelligence: Why it can matter more than I.Q.* New York: Bantam Books.

Hay, L. (2001). Thinking skills for the age of information. In A. Costa (Ed.), *Developing minds: A resource book for teaching thinking.* Alexandria, VA: Association for Supervision and Curriculum Development.

Helping students become self-directed learners. (1997). [Video course]. Santa Monica, CA: Canter & Associates, Inc.

Kuhn, T. S. (1962). *The structure of scientific revolutions.* Chicago: University of Chicago Press.

Laborde, G., & Saunders, C. (1986). *Communication trainings: Are they cost effective?* Mountain View, CA: International Dialogue Education Associates.

Lambert, L. (2003). *Leadership capacity for lasting school improvement.* Alexandria, VA: Association for Supervision and Curriculum Development.

Lambert, L., Walker, D., Zimmerman, D., Cooper, J., Gardner, M., Lambert, M. D., & Szabo, M. (2002). *The constructivist leader* (2nd ed.). New York: Teachers College Press.

Leonard, G. (1978). *The silent pulse. A search for the perfect rhythm that exists in each of us.* New York: Bantam.

Levy, S. (1996). *Starting from scratch: One classroom builds its own curriculum.* Portsmouth, NH: Heinemann.

Luft, J. (1984). *Group process: An introduction to group dynamics* (3rd ed.). Palo Alto, CA: Mayfield.

Marzano, R. (2001). *Designing a new taxonomy of educational objectives.* Thousand Oaks, CA: Corwin Press.

Maslow, A. (1968). *Toward a psychology of being.* New York: Harper.

Newcomb, A. (2003, May). Peter Senge on organizational learning. *The School Administrator Web Edition.* Retrieved May 2003, from http://www.aasa.org/publications/sa/2003_05SengeQ&A

Panella, M. (1997). Designing learning for a work environment: Key values and skills. In A. Costa & R. Liebmann (Eds.), *The process centered school: Sustaining a renaissance community.* Thousand Oaks, CA: Corwin Press.

Perkins, D. (1985). What creative thinking is. In A. L. Costa (Ed.), *Developing minds: A resource book for teaching thinking* (pp. 85-88). Alexandria, VA: Association for Supervision and Curriculum Development.

Perkins, D. (1995). Outsmarting IQ: The emerging science of learnable intelligence. New York: Free Press.

Perkins, D. (2001). The social side of thinking. In A. Costa (Ed.), *Developing minds: A resource book for teaching thinking.* Alexandria, VA: Association for Supervision and Curriculum Development.

Piaget, J. (1969). *Psychology of intelligence.* Totowa, NJ: Littlefield, Adams.

Resnick, L. (2001). Making America smarter: The real goal of school reform. In A. Costa (Ed.), *Developing minds: A resource book for teaching thinking.* Alexandria, VA: Association for Supervision and Curriculum Development.

Sanford, C. (1995). *Myths of organizational effectiveness at work.* Battle Ground, WA: Springhill.

Sawyer, L. (2003). Applying cognitive coaching to a framework for teaching. In J. Ellison & C. Hayes (Eds.), *Weaving the principles of cognitive coaching throughout the organization.* Norwood, MA: Christopher-Gordon.

Schlechty, P. (1997). *Inventing better schools: An action plan for educational reform.* San Francisco: Jossey-Bass.

Schön, D.A. (1983). *The reflective practioner: How professionals think in action.* New York: Basic Books.

Seiger-Eherenberg, S. (1991). Educational outcomes for a K-12 curriculum. In A. Costa (Ed.), *Developing minds: A resource book for teaching thinking.* Alexandria, VA: Association for Supervision and Curriculum Development.

Senge, P. (1990). The leader's new work: Building learning organizations. *Sloan Management Review* (Fall), 7-23.

Senge, P. (1997). Foreword. In A. Costa & R. Liebmann (Eds.), *Envisioning process as content.* Thousand Oaks, CA: Corwin Press.

Senge, P. (2003). Peter Senge on organizational learning. *The School Administrator Web Edition.* May 2003. Available at http://www.aasa.org/publications/sa/2003_05sengeq&A.htm

Senge, P., Ross, R., Smith, B., Roberts, C., & Kleiner, A. (1994). *The fifth discipline fieldbook.* New York: Doubleday/Currency.

Sigel, I. E. (1984). A constructivist perspective for teaching thinking. *Educational Leadership, 42*(3), 18-22.

Taba, H. (1962). *Curriculum development: Theory and practice.* New York: Harcourt Brace and World.

Vygotsky, L. S. (1978). *Mind in society: The development of higher psychological processes.* Cambridge, MA: Harvard University Press.

Wheatley, M., & Kellner-Rogers, M. (1998). A *simpler way.* San Francisco: Berrett-Kohler.

Wittrock, M. (1986). *Handbook of research on teaching* (3rd ed.). New York: Macmillan.

INDEX

CORWIN PRESS

The Corwin Press logo—a raven striding across an open book—represents the happy union of courage and learning. We are a professional-level publisher of books and journals for K-12 educators, and we are committed to creating and providing resources that embody these qualities. Corwin's motto is "Success for All Learners."

Printed in the USA
CPSIA information can be obtained
at www.ICGtesting.com
LVHW010744031123
762613LV00007B/44